ABOVE AND BEYOND
TRUE STORIES OF REAL HEROES

KEN OSMOND

Above And Beyond

Copyright © 2014 Ken Osmond
Edited by Kate Stewart
Cover Design by Digital Donna
Formatting by IRONHORSE Formatting
All Rights Reserved

This book is based upon real events and individuals. The author has done his best to make sure that the stories are told as accurately as possible.

ISBN-13: 978-0-615-97252-7

Dedication

This book is dedicated to the countless men and women that have worn their country's uniform, and so many who didn't wear one, but were willing to give their all, to protect the freedom that we have today.

Contents

Acknowledgments	i
Forward	1
Eugene Morgan	3
Mitchell Red Cloud	7
James Hoyt Jr.	10
Frank Day	13
Thomas J. Hudner	15
Eric Dowling	18
Doris Miller	21
Unknown	23
Max Warshaw	26
Ed Freeman	29
Wally Bludworth	32
Presley O'Bannon	35
Kenneth Reusser	38
John Basilone	41
Eddie Heimberger	44
Charles Angelo Liteky	46

Jack Rose	49
Knut Haugland	52
Jimmie Walters Monteith Jr.	55
Louis Stamatakos	58
Howard Benthine	61
Ian Fortune	64
Charles L. Brown	66
Eddie O'Hare	69
Walker Melville Mahurin	72
Edward A. Carter	75
Tibor Rubin	78
Eileen Nearne	81
Stubby	84
Salvatore Giunta	87
Channing Moss	90
Hershel Williams	93
Guy Louis Gabaldon	96
Dr. Lawton E. Shank	99
Robert Lewis Howard	102
Harvey Barnum	105

Matt Urban	108
Roland Wolfe	111
Carl Lucas Norden	115
Nancy Wake	118
Dr. Albert Brown	122
George Edward Hunt	125
Margy Reed	129
Reckless	133
Chris Kyle	136
Irena Sendler	139
Van Thomas Barfoot	142
Raymond Buthe	146
Maureen Dunlop de Popp	149
The Barb	152
About the Author	156

Acknowledgments

Special thanks to:
Katie O'Brian for her help to illustrate these stories.
My elder son Eric, whose computer skills enabled me to assemble these stories.
Christopher J. Lynch, whose background in writing and knowledge of the publishing process, enabled me to put it all together.

Forward

Many of us know so little about the military. History at its best involves real people. No frills, no icing; just individuals who made a difference. *Above And Beyond* takes us into the heart and soul of some of our heroes.

And they are a varied group indeed. *Above And Beyond* is about the most decorated Jewish veteran of World War II, Max Warshaw. We see Eddie Heimberger, who saved the lives of countless American marines long before he became a well-known actor, and Father Charles Liteky, a chaplain who dragged wounded soldiers to safety. The combat medals and awards of the son of Al Capone's lawyer, are displayed at Chicago's huge airport. Private Edward Carter received his Medal of Honor fifty years late. Martha Raye served as both an entertainer, and a nurse, to our troops.

A Los Angeles boy, Guy Gabaldon, was raised by a Japanese family until the household was sent to an internment camp. While serving in the Pacific, he became known as the Pied Piper of Saipan, after speaking with Japanese soldiers in their own language, and inducing them into surrendering. Years after serving, Van Thomas Barfoot, a Medal of Honor recipient, had to fight off his own homeowners association for his right to display the American flag.

While most of the heroes were born in the U.S.A., some were born elsewhere. A Hungarian man was liberated by American soldiers from Mauthausen Concentration Camp, only to later become an American soldier serving in Korea, and liberated once again from a prisoner of war camp. Others came from Norway, Scotland, England, the Netherlands, Argentina, and Poland.

Not all those who served were human. The first K9 hero, a pit bull named Stubby, saved the lives of many American soldiers in the trenches of France during World War I. A horse was made a US Marine Sergeant for her actions in Korea.

At the end of *Above And Beyond*, author Ken Osmond writes that if one cries while reading his book, "I've done my job." You certainly have done your job, Ken. And by the way, every time you wrote about someone in Vietnam, my heart thumped as I wondered whether or not I treated him while serving as a combat nurse at the 85th Evacuation Hospital in Qui Nhon Hospital.

From one soldier to another, thank you.

~Eileen Moore, R.N.
(Formerly stationed at the 85th evacuation Hospital, Qui Nhon, South Vietnam.)

EUGENE MORGAN

In August 1945, *Little Boy* completed its journey from New Mexico to Hiroshima. It was on the 6th, that the *Enola Gay* left Tinian with *Little Boy* aboard, on the final leg of that journey. It was the beginning of the end.

For many reasons, the assorted components of the device were transported separately to Tinian by various routes and methods.

Little Boy

The USS Indianapolis, a cruiser, delivered one of the major components. The Indianapolis left from Leyte, in the Philippines, with its precious cargo. Because of the need for secrecy and speed, she sailed unescorted.

USS Indianapolis

Mission accomplished; now they could return to Leyte. The 1196 members of her crew completed their assignment, without knowing what they had delivered.

On July 30, near the Marianas, a Japanese I-58 submarine spotted the cruiser, and fired six torpedoes at her. Two of the torpedoes found their mark, ripping her starboard side open. Boatswain Mate Second Class Eugene Morgan was asleep when the torpedoes exploded.

The order to abandon ship was given. Somehow, Morgan made it topside and into the water. In just twelve minutes, the Indianapolis disappeared beneath the surface.

Morgan scanned the debris for something to keep himself afloat. Spotting a floating crate of food, he swam toward it. It was then that he felt a shark rip the flesh off his back. Although critically injured, he managed to reach the container, and he climbed onto it. Sharks attacked many other sailors, most of them fatally. The sailors floated in the shark-infested water for five days. When help finally arrived, only 317 crewmembers had survived. When the war ended, Morgan returned to Seattle and became a firefighter. He never spoke of the tragedy.

Four decades later, Morgan's grandson, Jason Witty, joined the navy, and became a submariner aboard the USS Ohio. It was not until then, that Morgan related his ordeal to his grandson.

On October 2 of 2007 the Ohio surfaced at the location of the Indianapolis' tragedy. Three sailors formed on deck as an Honor Guard. Machinist First

Class Jason Witty emerged from the hatch to fulfill his grandfather's last wish. As the Honor Guard fired a salute, Jason spread the cremated remains of his grandfather onto the calm surface, and Boatswain Mate Second Class Eugene Morgan rejoined his shipmates.

Hand Salute----------Ready, Two

MITCHELL RED CLOUD

Very few of us have ever heard of the Ho-Chunk Indian Nation of American Indians of Wisconsin. After reading of Mitchell Red Cloud you will, because of his contribution to our freedom.

Born July 2, 1924 on the reservation in Hatfield, Wisconsin his youth was uneventful. In August of 1941, at sixteen years of age, he dropped out of school and joined the marines.

On November 4, 1942 the 2nd Battalion, 9th Marines which included Mitchell, was given the task of silencing the Japanese artillery that was firing on Henderson Field in Guadalcanal. They not only stopped the shelling, but they destroyed enemy supply and communication lines. Having contracted malaria and jaundice, Mitchell was ordered home and offered a medical discharge, which he declined.

He was reassigned to the 6th Marine Division and sent to Okinawa, where a shoulder wound earned him a Purple Heart. Red Cloud received an honorable discharge in 1946.

After two years of civilian life, he joined the army. At the outbreak of the Korean Conflict, he was sent to Korea with the 24th Infantry Regiment. Corporal Red Cloud often traded his rations for his comrades' candy, which he gave to Korean children. At twenty-five years old, he was the "old man" of E Company. Being a combat veteran, he was well respected. Red Cloud was the point man when a surprise attack by the North Koreans threatened his entire company. His relentless fire from his Browning automatic rifle held off the attack long enough for his company to take cover. This resulted in his being wounded several times. A medic treated him, but his company needed time to withdraw. He pulled himself up by holding onto a tree, and resumed firing, which gave his comrades the time to withdraw to safety.

In the morning, they found that eight additional rounds had ended this American's life.

In April 1951, General Omar Bradley presented a Medal of Honor to Red Cloud's mother.

Mitchell Red Cloud

On August 7, 1999 Kenneth Kershaw, a member of Red Cloud's company, was present at the launching of USNS Red Cloud, a strategic sealift ship. Kershaw said that if it hadn't been for Red Cloud's actions, he wouldn't be there.

Hand Salute----------Ready, Two

JAMES HOYT JR.

May 16, 1925 was an uneventful day for most, but in Oxford, Iowa railroad worker James Hoyt, and his schoolteacher wife, gave birth to James Jr.

At the outbreak of World War II, James Jr., like so many, felt the need to protect his country, and joined the army. He was attached to the 6th Armored Division, and deployed to the European Theater.

James had already been awarded a Bronze Star during the Battle of the Bulge. Now, his company was pushing deep into Germany. Many German units were surrendering, knowing their war was lost. Some of those spoke of a prison camp nearby. James and three others, Frederic Keffer, Herbert Gottschalk, and Harry Ward were sent to check it out.

On April 11, 1945 at nineteen years of age, he and his three comrades emerged from underbrush and were sickened by the discovery of one of the largest death camps ever built by the Nazis. James was the first to cut through the fence, and was greeted with incredible exuberance by the emaciated prisoners. He saw mountains of dead bodies, fifteen to twenty feet high, as well as other unspeakable atrocities. The report of the four men resulted in the liberation of the 21,000 prisoners in the camp.

It wasn't long before the war ended. Despite all that he had experienced, he was able to lead a normal life. James delivered mail in his hometown for thirty years, but the haunting memories of the unspeakable atrocities he witnessed that day at Buchenwald stayed with him the rest of his life, requiring weekly therapy for years.

On August 11, 2008 Doris, whom he married in 1949, was handed a folded American flag by General Robert Sentman (Retired). The flag had been carefully folded twelve times by a Color Guard. The horrific dreams James experienced since that day at Buchenwald finally ended.

Buchenwald

America had lost another hero.

Hand Salute----------Ready, Two

FRANK DAY

On March 24, 1944 allied POWs made a daring escape from Stalag Luft III inside German lines.

We have all seen this story brought to life in the movie, *The Great Escape*.

When I first saw the movie, I remember how sorry I felt for the man at the end of the tunnel when the Germans discovered it. He was so close to freedom, but was forced to return back through the 330-foot tunnel into the camp. His name was Frank Day. As it turned out, my sympathy was misplaced. Almost all the escapees were recaptured. Only a few were returned to the camp. Over fifty were shot.

Born May 5, 1917 in Chiswick, England, Frank Day became a member of the Royal Air Force. While flying a Spitfire on a reconnaissance mission over the Aegean Sea he was attacked by several Messerschmitts. His knee was shattered, he lost his thumb, and was forced to bail out. After floating in the sea for twenty-four hours, he was captured.

Had Frank Day made it out of the camp, his plan was to steal a plane from a nearby airfield and fly to freedom. James Garner depicted him in the movie.

In May 1945, the camp was liberated and he was returned to England.

On his ninetieth birthday, he was honored with a flyby of vintage spitfires for being the oldest living "caterpillar" and "penguin", which are the respective nicknames of pilots saved by parachute, and pilots adrift in the sea.

Frank Day

Frank Day passed away on June 29, 2008.

Hand Salute----------Ready, Two

THOMAS J. HUDNER

Thomas J. Hudner was born into an affluent family in Fall River, Massachusetts. He was raised in a privileged manner that would be fitting a child of his social position, attending the most prestigious schools, including the U.S. Naval Academy. He served for two years before entering naval flight school. He received his "wings of gold" in 1949.

At the outbreak of the Korean Conflict, Lieutenant J.G. Hudner found himself part of an eight Corsair group flying armed reconnaissance flights near the Chosin Reservoir. His wingman was Ensign Jesse L. Brown.

Brown was born and raised at the opposite end of the economic and social hierarchy, a black man from Mississippi with a minimal education. Regardless, they had become friends.

On Dec. 4, 1950 while on patrol looking for targets of opportunity, they were receiving small arms fire when Brown's Corsair suffered a severed oil line. It's speculated it was just a "lucky" shot. At only 1000 feet, there was little Brown could do. His Corsair slammed into the ground. He survived, but was pinned inside the smoldering wreck. It would take fifteen minutes for the rescue helicopter to reach the site.

Hudner saw a communist patrol making their way toward the wreckage. Without hesitation, he "pancaked" his plane about 100 yards from Brown. Hudner found that Brown's leg was crushed and trapped inside the cockpit. He was unable to free the leg. He could do nothing but stand guard. When the helicopter arrived, they found that the leg was hopelessly trapped. Hudner and the rescue pilot were about to amputate Brown's leg as a last resort in order to evacuate him, when they heard his final gasp. Ensign Jesse Brown was dead.

President Harry Truman and Lieutenant J.G. Thomas Hudner

April 13, 1951 Jesse Brown's widow, Daisy, was present when President Harry Truman presented Lieutenant J.G. Thomas Hudner with the Medal of Honor.

Hand Salute----------Ready, Two

ERIC DOWLING

Eric Dowling was born on July 22, 1915 in Glastonbury, a town of 8800 in the south west of England. Eric's mother died when he was only thirteen years old and he was sent to a boarding school.

After finishing his schooling, he returned to Glastonbury, until the outbreak of World War II. Like so many of his countrymen, he felt compelled to do his part in fighting the spread of the Third Reich. He joined the Royal Air Force, known as the RAF, and was trained as a navigator. He was assigned to the 57th Fighter Group, a squadron aboard a Wellington bomber.

Eric completed twenty-nine missions over Germany before a fateful April day when his plane was shot down over enemy territory and he was taken prisoner by the Germans. They sent him to Stalag Luft III, the now infamous POW camp depicted in the movie *The Great Escape*. The camp was intended to house British airmen, but with the growing number of POWs, the Germans began confining other allied prisoners with different types of training as well. Fortunately, among them was a mining engineer, who would later be instrumental in the digging of the three escape tunnels nicknamed, "Tom, Dick, and Harry".

When the escape plot was devised, they planned on getting 250 men out of the camp, and drew that many names out of a hat. Eric's name was not among the lucky ones. He was not disheartened by this however, and worked hard to help the success of the plot. He spent his time in incarceration learning five languages. He taught the fortunate ones on the list, phrases in German that might help them. He helped convert uniforms into civilian clothing, and did most of the forging of fake German documents. When "Dick" collapsed, and "Tom" was discovered, Eric dug constantly to complete "Harry", earning him the nickname of "Digger".

Seventy-six men escaped through the tunnel before the Germans discovered it. Most were caught; fifty were executed by machine gun.

Only a few made their way to freedom. Eric spent the rest of the war in Stalag Luft III.

With the end of the war, the camp was liberated, and Eric returned to England where he became an accident investigator for the UK Civil Aviation Authority, the British equivalent of the FAA.

Flight Lieutenant Eric "Digger" Dowling made his final escape one day before his ninety-third birthday.

Flight Lieutenant Eric "Digger" Dowling

Hand Salute----------Ready, Two

DORIS MILLER

Cory Miller's father had been a slave when Lincoln was president. Life was hard on Cory, but he and his wife, Henrietta, had managed to buy a small farm near Waco, Texas. On October 12, 1919 they had a son, Doris.

On September 16, 1939 Doris joined the Navy to help support his parents. There were very few positions open to a black man in the Navy in 1939. He was trained as a mess attendant. Doris didn't even receive basic combat training. He was assigned to the USS West Virginia.

On that "date in infamy", Doris awoke to the sound of: *General Quarters*.

He ran topside and began carrying wounded sailors to more sheltered areas. An officer ordered him to the bridge to attend the wounded captain, but the captain was dead. Doris mounted a .50 caliber Browning anti-aircraft machine gun, and was credited with the downing of a Japanese fighter. He later said, "I didn't know what I was doing, I just pulled the trigger, and it worked."

Mess Attendant Third Class Doris (Dorie) Miller

As the West Virginia was lost, Doris was reassigned to the USS Liscome Bay.

On November 24, 1943 in the Tarawa Atolls, a Japanese submarine fired a single torpedo, striking the Liscome Bay near the stern. The aircraft bomb magazine exploded. Only 272 sailors survived. Doris "Dorie" Miller was not among them.

Mess Attendant Third Class Doris "Dorie" Miller had earned a Purple Heart and the Navy Cross.

Commissioned on June 30, 1973 the Knox-class frigate USS Miller was named in his honor.

Hand Salute----------Ready, Two

Unknown

The Department of the Navy honors the "best of the best" with their highest decoration, the Navy Cross, for valor "above and beyond" under hostile fire, second only to the Medal of Honor. There have been 6924 Navy Crosses awarded. In 2003, that number rose by one. When the Department of the Navy released the citation, much of the facts about the recipient and his mission were deleted due to the sensitive nature of the mission. This unnamed naval medical officer can't wear it or display it.

The recipient was part of a mounted patrol with Afghan personnel. The patrol was ambushed with heavy enemy fire. The lieutenant returned fire and pulled the wounded Afghan commander from the truck. He then exposed himself to enemy fire in order to extricate a wounded American from another truck.

He then pulled yet another wounded American from the truck. Using his body as a shield, he treated these wounded men. In so doing, several enemy rounds struck him but were stopped by his body armor. Still under fire, he checked the other vehicle for additional wounded. He found two, removed them, and treated their wounds.

The lieutenant then rallied a group of Afghan soldiers that were in a state of disarray, and was able to break the ambush.

Later that same day, he was part of a combined US/Afghan element sweeping the area of the earlier ambush, when a platoon-sized enemy force attacked them. An American and an Afghan were wounded. The lieutenant ran 200 meters between opposing forces, under heavy machine gun fire, to treat the two men.

While treating them, he received several shrapnel wounds. He mustered the remaining Afghans and led a fighting withdrawal. The unit returned to their base camp before he treated his own wounds.

Someday we'll know your name and you can wear your richly deserved Navy Cross.

Hand Salute----------Ready, Two

MAX WARSHAW

In December 1913, Blanch and Jacob Warshaw added Max to the Jewish community in Korbin, Poland.

Ten Years later, like so many Europeans seeking opportunity, the three of them immigrated to the United States. Max was educated in the New York public school system.

When the United States entered World War II, Max felt he had to do his part, but he also knew he would be unable to take a human life. He joined the army, and was trained to be a medic. His newly formed division was sent to North Africa. On November 8, 1942 during a fierce battle in Oran, Algeria he repeatedly exposed himself to enemy fire to rescue wounded comrades from open areas. Max was rewarded with a Bronze Star. Just two days later, on November 10, he was wounded by an artillery round. He remained on duty, but had shrapnel removed several times over several years.

March 25, 1943 near El Guettar, Tunisia he subjected himself to heavy artillery fire to retrieve two abandoned US trucks loaded with much needed supplies. He received the Silver Star for this act.

Max was among the first wave to land on Omaha Beach on D-day. He received his second Bronze Star for heroism for his actions on June 14 and 15. He received his third Bronze Star for similar acts he carried out on October 13, this time in his native country of Poland. Just three days later, for "gallantry beyond the call of duty" he received his second Silver Star.

On November 25, 1944 he was captured by Germans, and spent the duration of the war as a POW.

When he returned to his wife Evelyn, in Fair Lawn, New Jersey he also brought with him, a Purple Heart, Ex Prisoner of War Medal, European-African-Middle Eastern Campaign Medal with six campaign clusters, World War II Victory Medal, Conspicuous Cross Medal, and the Combat Medical Badge.

Most Decorated Jewish Veteran of World War II

He never carried a gun, or took a human life, but he was the most decorated Jewish veteran of World War II. He was Polish, but this was a real American.

Hand Salute----------Ready, Two

ED FREEMAN

Ed Freeman wanted to do his part to save America from Adolf Hitler, but he was still too young when the war ended. When he was old enough, he joined the army to do his part, even though it was peacetime.

By the time the Korean Conflict broke out, he was a master sergeant and fought as an infantryman. Sergeant Freeman had been in several heated battles, but was put to the test on the infamous "Pork Chop Hill". He passed that test so well, that he received a battlefield commission. This commission enabled him to apply for flight training, which had been a lifelong dream. Lieutenant Freeman was told that at six foot four he was too tall. The nickname "Too Tall" stuck with him the rest of his career. In 1955, the height limit was removed, and he earned his wings. He loved the flying, but he found his real passion when he moved to helicopters.

Huey

In 1965, he had flown thousands of hours in helicopters and was sent to Vietnam as part of the 1st Cavalry Division. He was second in command of a sixteen-helicopter unit. On November 14 of that year, his unit carried a battalion into the Ia Drang Valley for what became the first major confrontation with the North Vietnamese Army (NVA) regulars. Back at base, he learned that the troops they had carried into battle were suffering heavy casualties, and were low on ammunition. Fighting was so fierce that the infantry commander ordered medi-vac choppers not to land. Too Tall and one other, volunteered to try. Loaded with ammunition, they landed their unarmed ships in the middle of the battle. They were on the ground just long enough to fill their Hueys with wounded and evacuate them. This was not enough for Too Tall. He returned for a second load, and then a third.

Captain Ed "Too Tall" Freeman made fourteen landings during the heated battle, evacuating thirty wounded men. For this, he received the Distinguished Flying Cross. Those thirty men were not satisfied. A campaign was mounted, and in July of 2001, President Bush placed a Medal of Honor around the neck of Too Tall.

On August 20, 2008 Ed Freeman passed away in Boise, Idaho.

Hand Salute----------Ready, Two

WALLY BLUDWORTH

Wally Bludworth was a small-town boy born and raised in Kyle, Texas. He had watched his father join the army several years before World War II. When the war broke out in Europe, his father became a tail gunner on a B-17. Wally's grandfather had helped defeat the Kaiser as a marine in World War I. In 1944, Wally was old enough to help his father defeat Hitler, and he joined the Army Air Corps. He became a pilot on a B-24, a successor to what his father had flown.

B-24

Flight crews earned "points" for each mission they flew over enemy territory. After twenty-five missions, they had enough "points" to rotate back to the US. On 19 of his missions, Wally returned to England on only one engine, or with the controls shot up. Like all the other flight crews, Captain Bludworth anxiously counted his missions: 23, 24, 25, 26, 27, and was still being sent into harm's way. On one of his flights, his plane was shot down over German-occupied Belgium. He sought concealment from the Germans in an abandoned schoolhouse, where he slept for several days. When the 2nd Armored Division routed the Germans from the small town, he was liberated and returned to his base in England. He celebrated his twenty-first birthday by bombing Berlin. By the time Germany was defeated, Captain Bludworth had flown thirty-four missions.

On March 10, 2009 the governor of Texas honored Wally Bludworth by treating him to a flight to Austin in the only flying B-24 still in existence. When they landed in Austin, Wally Bludworth was decorated with a Distinguished Flying Cross, which had been authorized on December 1, 1945 but had never been presented.

Hand Salute----------Ready, Two

Presley O'Bannon

When the USS Philadelphia ran aground off the north coast of Africa, the real problem was not damage to the ship, or the fear of sinking, but that the ship had been taken over by the enemy and the crew was taken prisoner. They were being held in the port city of Darna, inaccessible by land and well fortified against attack from the sea. It was decided that a small force of marines could make the 500-mile overland trek from Alexandra. Enlisting the help of sympathetic tribesman along the route, an attack could be launched from the undefended landward side.

The task fell on 29-year-old Marine Lieutenant Presley O'Bannon. With one navy midshipman and seven marines, he began what would turn out to be a forty-five day march to Darna.

Lieutenant O'Bannon, along with approximately 500 of the volunteer tribesman, led an all-out attack on the headquarters of the enemy. They were able to silence the massive guns defending the harbor.

This allowed the three American ships; the USS Argus, USS Hornet, and the USS Nautilus, to enter the harbor to complete the victory and secure the city. The prisoners were liberated.

This was not without a high cost. Two of the marines, Private John Whitten and Private Edward Steweard paid the ultimate cost to secure our freedom.

Lieutenant Presley O'Bannon
"To the shores of Tripoli"

The date was April 27, 1805. The enemy was pirates. The allies were Egyptian tribesman. The country was Tripoli, known today as Libya. This was the first time the American flag flew on foreign soil. "To the shores of Tripoli."

Semper Fi

Hand Salute----------Ready, Two

KENNETH REUSSER

His first parachute jump was as a child from the roof of the barn with a bed sheet. It would not be his last. Kenneth Reusser earned his pilot's license before the outbreak of World War II. When America got involved, he became a Marine Corps aviator.

In 1945, while he was stationed in Okinawa, the Japanese were using a Kawasaki "Dragon Killer" airplane to photograph US preparations to invade Japan. The Kawasaki flew higher than our Corsairs normally could. Reusser stripped his Corsair to the bone, and went hunting at 40,000 feet. He found the Kawasaki, and attacked, only to discover his machine guns were frozen. He closed in on the Kawasaki from the rear, and destroyed the vertical stabilizer with his prop. The enemy went down, and he limped back to base with a damaged prop.

In 1950, he found himself in a different war. Now a major, but still in a Corsair, he was leading the famous "Black Sheep Squadron" and flying missions over Inchon from the deck of the USS Sicily. On one of his missions, they were unable to locate the reported arms factory that was to be their target. Major Reusser made a run between the buildings that was low enough to see Soviet tanks through the windows. He returned to the Sicily long enough to refuel and rearm. He then destroyed the "factory" with rockets and napalm. While returning to the Sicily, he spotted a camouflaged oil tanker in Inchon harbor. At mast height, he strafed the tanker with 20mm gunfire. The tanker exploded, almost blowing the Corsair out of the air.

By the time the US got involved in Vietnam, Reusser had given up the Corsair in favor of a Huey helicopter. He was leading a marine helicopter group on a rescue mission when his Huey was shot down, resulting in him being burned over thirty-five percent of his body. Eventually, he was forced to retire as a result of these injuries. These are only a sample of the things this man did for America.

Colonel Kenneth Reusser

On June 20, 2009 the now-retired Colonel Kenneth Reusser passed away peacefully. His life was less than peaceful. He fought in three wars, flew 253 combat missions, and was shot down five times. In all, he earned two Navy Crosses, five Purple Hearts, two Legions of Merit, and 42 other decorations. He remains the most decorated marine aviator in history.

Hand Salute----------Ready, Two

JOHN BASILONE

John Basilone was one of ten children born to Salvatore and Dora Basilone. His parents were first generation Italian immigrants and he was raised in Raritan, New Jersey. English was his second language.

In 1934, at eighteen years old, he joined the U.S. Army, and was sent to the Philippines, where he picked up the nickname, "Manila John". In 1937, he received an honorable discharge.

After serving three years in the army, Manila John had fulfilled his service to America, but anticipating the outbreak of World War II, in July 1940, he enlisted in the US Marines.

Over the two-day period of October 24 and 25 in 1942 Gunnery Sergeant Basilone was in charge of two sections of heavy machine guns. They were defending a narrow pass to Henderson Airfield on Guadalcanal. The small contingent of leathernecks was vastly outnumbered by the Japanese, who were making repeated assaults on their position. The machine gun on his left was knocked out. Manila John picked up the other 90-pound machine gun and ran 200 yards to the location of the destroyed weapon and started firing. Enemy soldiers attacked his rear. He cut them down with his pistol. Short of ammunition, he ran 200 yards through heavy fire to an ammo dump. He returned to his position and resumed firing. At dawn, they found thirty-eight enemy bodies.

The line was held and for this, he was awarded the Medal of Honor.

Sergeant Basilone was sent stateside to tour for the war bond effort. He even made the cover of *Life* magazine. He was a hero, but he insisted he was just a plain old marine like his buddies still fighting in the South Pacific.

Sergeant John Basilone

His request to return to his unit was granted. He caught up with his unit at Iwo Jima. On February 19, 1945 under heavy artillery fire, he single-handedly took out an enemy blockhouse. Minutes later, an enemy artillery round took the lives of five heroic marines, including Manila John. He was posthumously awarded the Navy Cross and the Purple Heart.

Today, Sergeant John Basilone is at peace in section 12, Site 384, Arlington National Cemetery.

Hand Salute----------Ready, Two

EDDIE HEIMBERGER

Halfway between Hawaii and Australia, lies an atoll too small to even qualify as an island. Although Tarawa is smaller that Manhattan's Central Park, it was important from a military point of view, because it had an airfield which could extend the range of air strikes against the Japanese. Tarawa was under Japanese control since it had been taken from the British on December 10, 1941.

For three days in November 1942, America bombarded the tiny atoll with 2000 tons of shells from ships, and 900 tons of bombs from the air. Now, putting boots on the ground would be a "piece of cake". Wrong. The next three days would prove just how wrong. The marines attempting to invade this tiny atoll experienced one of the bloodiest battles of the Pacific campaign.

On the second day of the battle, Lieutenant Eddie Heimberger was operating a salvage boat, which was to collect equipment from the beach for repair and reuse. Lieutenant Heimberger discovered scores of wounded marines trapped on the barrier reef that encircled the atoll. The Lieutenant began picking up the wounded from the reef, and making many trips between the reef and a transport ship. These trips saved the lives of dozens of marines. For his actions, he was awarded the Bronze Star.

After the war, he enjoyed a successful career as an actor, using the name Eddie Albert.

Eddie (Heimberger) Albert

The "piece of cake" cost the lives of 990 marines and 680 sailors, and 2300 others were wounded. The battle yielded four Medals of Honor, thirty-four Navy Crosses, and 250 Silver Stars.

Hand Salute----------Ready, Two

CHARLES ANGELO LITEKY

On February 14, 1931 our nation's capital saw the birth of Charles Angelo Liteky. From all accounts, Charles enjoyed a normal, uneventful childhood. What was different about Charles was that he knew at an early age where his life was going. He had a calling.

In 1960, Charles was ordained and became Father Liteky. Until then, he believed this was his calling. He was to find out that his calling was only beginning.

As the 1960s progressed, the war in Vietnam was heating up. The U.S. Army approached Father Liteky, and offered him a commission if he would help them with their shortage of Chaplains. Soon, Chaplain (Lieutenant) Liteky was on his way to Vietnam.

Chaplain (Lieutenant) Liteky lived down in the trenches and liked to be considered just another "grunt". He was well liked, and even heard confessions while on patrol.

By the time he was assigned to the 199th Infantry Brigade, he had made Captain.

On December 6, 1967 while on a "search and destroy", his company came under intense fire from a battalion-sized enemy force. Chaplain (Captain) Liteky saw two wounded men lying within fifteen meters of an enemy machine gun. He crawled to them and was able to drag both to an area of safety, before carrying them to the LZ, or landing zone.

Then, in a magnificent display of courage, he stood upright and moved through the enemy fire, administering last rites to the dying, and evacuating the wounded. He noticed another wounded man, and crawled to his aid. Realizing that this man was too heavy to carry, he rolled onto his back and placed the man on his own chest. Then, using his feet and elbows he pushed himself along until they reached the LZ. The Chaplain returned to the savage battle again and again evacuating wounded.

Only after the fighting was over and the enemy had been repelled, was it noticed that Chaplain Liteky had been wounded in the neck and foot. He had been able to evacuate twenty wounded men to the LZ.

Chaplain Charles Angelo Liteky

In November 1968, President Lyndon Johnson draped a Medal of Honor around Chaplain Liteky's neck, and was heard to say, "Son, I'd rather have one of these babies than be president".

Hand Salute----------Ready, Two

JACK ROSE

On January 18, 1917 in Blackheath, a small suburb of London, England welcomed Jack Rose into the world. After finishing his primary education, Jack attended University College in London. While studying science he found time to play on their rugby team.

In 1938, he joined the Royal Air Force Volunteer Reserve, where he earned his wings as a fighter pilot. War broke out for England. The RAF readied itself for the fight against Hitler. Among their preparations, each pilot was issued a pack of bright-green dye that would float on the waters of the English Channel if it became necessary to "ditch". This dye would help rescuers locate the downed pilot.

Rose borrowed an oversized needle and sewed the dye pack onto his flight jacket.

Jack Rose

On his first midair encounter with twelve German Dornier 215s, over the English Channel, his Hurricane was disabled and became uncontrollable. Rose was forced to bail out. After floating for two hours, his green dye was spotted and he was rescued. He learned later that another member of his flight group had also ditched. Since he had not sewn on his dye pack, however, he was never located.

On May 14, 1940 the Germans broke through allied lines at Sedan, a small town six miles south of the Belgian border. German bombers, and their fighter escorts, were causing massive casualties to ground forces. The RAF's No. 56 Squadron and the No. 3 Squadron, where Jack Rose served, were called into the battle. For four days the battle was intense. Jack was credited with the downing of two Messerschmitt Bf 109 fighters. Later that afternoon, he learned that his brother Tommy, a part of the 56 Squadron had been shot down and killed in the same battle. The very next day, he was able to get close to the rear of a Heinkel HE-111 bomber. He fired. The Heinkel's left engine blew up, covering the windshield of Rose's Hurricane with oil. Rose was effectively blind. He slowed his aircraft and unfastened his harness. Standing in the seat, he wiped the oil from the windshield.

At that moment, tracers began ripping into his Hurricane. Rose was able to control the plane and landed safely. Later, the German attacker, on seeing Rose standing in the aircraft seat, had reported the pilot was preparing to bail out, and took credit for the "kill".

Rose flew many flights over northern France with Czech and Polish squadrons. In October of 1942, he was awarded the Distinguished Flying Cross. He continued flying combat missions until Germany was defeated. Later, he was sent to the Asian Theater of the war, and flew many missions over Burma.

The end of the war credited Rose credited as one of the few pilots to survive flying on the first and last days of the war.

On October 10, 2009 Jack Rose passed away peacefully in his hometown of Blackheath.

Hand Salute----------Ready, Two

KNUT HAUGLAND

If you're a "baby boomer", you might remember the 1950 Oscar-winning documentary, *Kon-Tiki*. It depicted the adventurous 1947 sailing of a balsa-wood raft from Callao, Peru to Polynesia by a six-man crew. The only modern technology they had onboard was a hand-cranked radio to keep the world informed of their progress. The radio operator was Knut Haugland.

Knut had been trained in radio technology in his native Norway. After Hitler overran Norway in 1940, Knut took on the appearance of a docile factory worker in Oslo, when in fact he was a major figure in the Norwegian resistance movement.

Kon-Tiki

The movement was helpful, but its forces were scattered as they were operating as many individual groups. The British Special Operations Executive (SOE) stepped in to help them form a network with radio communications. This network, the British reasoned, would allow the movement to work together as a team. Knut's job was to build, repair, steal, or otherwise procure radios, and get them to the many small units of resistance.

He fought with the underground until August 1941, when the Germans arrested him. Knut was able to escape, and joined another Norwegian resistance group. This group was under the direction of the British. While fighting alongside this group, he was captured two more times, but was able to escape both times. One of their attacks against the Germans was made into a 1965 movie, *The Heroes of Telemark*, staring Kirk Douglas. The purpose of that attack was to sabotage a "heavy water" plant. This product is used in the development of atomic weapons. This sabotage prevented the Germans from beating the US in the development of the atomic bomb.

He continued to fight with the resistance until the 1945 liberation of Norway.

Knut Haugland passed away on Christmas 2009, at the age of 92.

Hand Salute----------Ready, Two

JIMMIE WALTERS MONTEITH JR.

Jimmie Walters Monteith Jr. was born July 1, 1917. A homegrown Virginia boy, he was raised in Low Moor and raised with hometown values of right and wrong.

In high school, he played on both the varsity football and varsity basketball teams. From 1937 to 1939, he attended Virginia Polytechnic Institute majoring in mechanical engineering. After school, he went to work as a field representative for Cable Coal Company.

In October of 1941, he was drafted into the army and sent to Camp Croft, South Carolina. While still in basic training, he was promoted to Corporal. Corporal Monteith applied for, and was accepted to, Officer Candidate School. In April of 1943, Second Lieutenant Monteith was shipped to Algeria to join the 1st Marine Division, also known as The Big Red One. The division moved on to Sicily and before the end of the year, Jimmie Monteith received a field promotion to First Lieutenant. In November of '44, the division moved to England to prepare for "the invasion".

June 6, 1944 D-day: The invasion was underway with the Big Red One leading the first assault at Normandy beach. Monteith was part of that first assault. Under heavy fire, he continually moved up and down the beach reorganizing the troops. He led the assault over a narrow exposed ridge. He retraced his path across the beach to two buttoned-up and blind tanks, which had been stopped by a minefield. Clearing a path for the tanks, he led them to a location where their guns could be used effectively. Under violent enemy fire, he led attack after attack, and was instrumental in the capture of several key enemy positions.

June 6, 1944 was a great victory for the allies, but was paid for with many lives. It is estimated to have cost over 2500 allied lives, including the life of First Lieutenant Jimmie Monteith Jr. Today he is at peace in the American Cemetery and Memorial, Normandy, France. Section 1, row 20, grave 12.

Lieutenant Jimmie Walters Monteith Jr.

His parents accepted his posthumous Medal of Honor.

Hand Salute----------Ready, Two

LOUIS STAMATAKOS

Had it not been for his three sons, Louis Stamatakos' actions of February 28, 1945 would have gone unrewarded.

Louis was born and raised in Dayton, Ohio. Dayton is often referred to as the birthplace of flight because Wilber and Orville Wright's bicycle shop was there. This may have contributed to Louis' fascination with flight.

At the outbreak of World War II, he joined the Army Air Corps and was trained as a tail gunner on the B-17, the Flying Fortress. By the end of the war, he had survived thirty-one successful missions, but his twenty-third was almost his last.

The crew of the "Miss BeHavin" had finished their bomb run of railroad yards in Kassel, Germany and were returning to England. They were unable to close the bomb bay doors. The navigator saw that two of the bombs had not been fully released and were dangling on their shackles. The bombs were half way out of the plane. The rushing wind had activated the small propellers on their nose thus arming the explosives. Someone yelled to "get the Greek", referring to Stamatakos, "he's been going to armament school." Louis grabbed a short-handled fire ax and straddled one of the bombs, à la Chill Wills, at an altitude of 20,000 feet and an air temp of -20 degrees. He beat on the bomb shackles until the ordinance broke free and fell away from the vessel. Crewmembers pulled him back into the safety of the plane.

Unbeknownst to their father, his sons; Philip, Timothy, and Ted located the navigator of the "Miss BeHavin", Richard Rainoldi, who was living in California. The four of them petitioned Congress, and on February 17, 2010 in the state capitol, Louis Stamatakos was decorated with a Silver Star.

Louis Stamatakos

Hand Salute----------Ready, Two

HOWARD BENTHINE

He didn't throw himself on a live hand grenade, or save twenty other men from certain death, or any other heroic thing they make movies about. He survived Leyte.

Howard Benthine was drafted into the army in April 1943. His service in New Guinea made him witness to unimaginable carnage on an island called Leyte, which is part of the Philippines. Leyte was all jungle fighting. He was just eighteen years old when he was forced to kill an enemy soldier. "I grabbed him by his head and snapped his neck. I immediately got sick, but I did what I was trained to do."

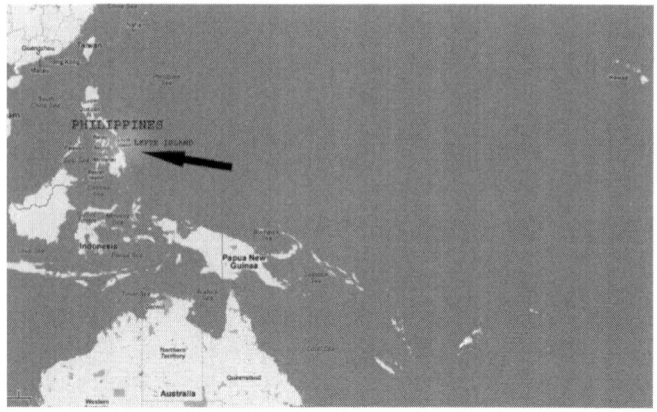

Howard Benthine first arrived in New Guinea in January of 1944. He was assigned with three other men to "intelligence" work. Their job was to go to the location of recent battles, to look for and retrieve written material that might contain useful information. The job included searching dead Japanese soldiers. Often the dead bodies had been rotting in the tropical jungle for several days.

It was common that his small unit was the target of sniper fire. Once a sniper round passed through his shirt. On one patrol, they looked down from the top of a hill and saw two Japanese soldiers sitting by a small fire. The two soldiers were eating one of their dead companions. Then one morning, his small team was sent to a place called the Driniumor River. The river is only about one foot deep and 125 feet wide. There had been several banzai attacks at the river two days before, each time the enemy was cut down by machine gun fire. Japanese bodies were two and three deep from bank to bank. He said you could walk from one side of the river to the other across the bodies without getting your feet wet. His job was to search them all.

By December of 1944, he had developed "jungle rot" which is a debilitating fungus caused by the island's swampy environment. He suffered from the rot for decades. Howard remained in that assignment until the end of the war. He said he got sick and vomited every day he was on the island. He was on Leyte until he was discharged in January 1946.

Upon his return home, he vowed that he would not give in to the haunting memories of carnage he had witnessed, even though they filled his dreams every night. He kept that vow and led a "normal" life. He worked for the Santa Fe Railway for thirty-nine years, and was married to Juanita for sixty-three years.

At 85 years old, his body was riddled with cancer, and he was forced to wear a colostomy bag. Once again, he had resigned himself to survive. "The damn Japs couldn't kill me. This cancer won't either." He was wrong. The cancer proved to be more determined than the "damn Japs". On April 10, 2010 the cancer took Howard Benthine.

Hand Salute----------Ready, Two

IAN FORTUNE

In January of 2010, a firefight was raging between American and heavily armed Afghan forces near Garmsir in Helmand Province. The Americans were suffering heavy casualties, and called for medevac helicopters to fly the wounded to safety.

Due to the large number of wounded, a Chinook was to be sent. A Chinook is a large twin rotor helicopter capable of a 12,000-pound payload. Flight Lieutenant Ian Fortune took off in the Chinook and headed for the firefight. A small news crew had flown with Lieutenant Fortune for the purpose of filming the rescue. The ground forces advised the helicopter to stay out of range due to the intensity of the Afghan attack. As the intensity of the attack lessoned, a landing was cleared.

Chinook Helicopter

The Chinook landed and twenty wounded soldiers were loaded onboard. Lieutenant Fortune had just lifted off when an enemy round pierced the windshield of the helicopter. The round then passed through the lieutenant's helmet and struck him between the eyes. Another round hit the Chinook's controls, shutting down the stabilization system. The pilot was nearly blind from the blood streaming down his face.

Without the stabilization system, he fought to keep the giant ship from spinning out of control. He had to constantly wipe the blood from his face so he could see. Fighting to maintain consciousness, he was able to make the 10-minute flight to the field hospital and land safely. His all-important cargo was safe.

Flight Lieutenant Ian Fortune will recover from his wounds.

Hand Salute----------Ready, Two

CHARLES L. BROWN

It was late in 1943 when newly commissioned Charles L. Brown earned his wings as a B-17 pilot. He was immediately sent to England to take command of a brand new Flying Fortress with a crew that was as green as he was. Tradition dictated that the commander of a new aircraft give the ship a name. "Ye Olde Pub" was given life.

On December 20, 1943 the virgin pilot, with a virgin crew, took off in the virgin Ye Olde Pub on their first combat mission. Their target was the heavily defended aircraft factory at Bremen, Germany.

During the bombing run, Ye Olde Pub was engulfed by anti-aircraft fire. She sustained massive damage.

The tail gunner lay dead in the aft of the plane. The turret gunner's body was spread over the top of the fuselage. Shrapnel hit Lieutenant Brown's right shoulder. Two other crewmembers were wounded.

One engine was dead and two others were damaged. The nose of the aircraft was blown off. The vertical stabilizer was gone, and the elevators were damaged. The worst part of the plane's damage was that the instrument panel had been destroyed. Ye Olde Pub was flying blind. She dropped out of formation.

Luftwaffe ace Franz Stigler in his Bf-109, closed in for the kill. As he got closer, he couldn't believe that a plane with such damage could still be flying. Stigler chose not to shoot down this defenseless aircraft, but instead, got alongside and signaled Lieutenant Brown to land. Brown refused.

"Ye Olde Pub"

Because the plane was flying deeper into enemy air space, Stigler realized they were flying blind. He signaled Brown to make a 180 degree turn and to follow him. Brown complied. Stigler led Ye Olde Pub out over the North Sea. He indicated to Brown the direction of England. Stigler saluted, turned, and returned to Europe. He later reported that the crippled B-17 had crashed into the North Sea.

Ye Olde Pub was able to make it back to their home base, but never flew again. Lieutenant Brown took command of the "Carol Dawn", and flew twenty-nine combat missions before Hitler was defeated.

After forty years, Charles Brown finally learned the name of that honorable Luftwaffe pilot. A meeting was arranged. In the late 1990s the two former pilots met. They stood face to face, and saluted each other. They had a brief, private conversation.

In 2008, both of these warriors peacefully passed away.

Hand Salute----------Ready, Two

Eddie O'Hare

Eddie O'Hare was a very smart St. Louis attorney, although many would say he was without personal values. Al Capone hired him as his full-time attorney. On many occasions, "Easy Eddie" was successful in keeping Capone out of prison. The one thing Eddie did value and love, was his son, Eddie Jr., whom he nicknamed Butch. His father got Butch into the prestigious Western Military Academy. Butch loved it and wanted to go on to the naval academy at Annapolis. In order to accomplish this for his son, Easy Eddie made a deal with the "Feds", and testified against Capone, exposing his tax evasion. Within a year, Butch was in Annapolis, and Easy Eddie was found shot to death in his car.

Graduating Annapolis in 1936, Lieutenant Eddie "Butch" O'Hare was required to serve two years on a surface ship, the USS New Mexico, before he could attend pilot training. It wasn't long before he was aboard the USS Lexington, as a carrier-based Wildcat pilot sailing into the South Pacific Theater of World War II.

Returning from a patrol flight, O'Hare and his wingman spotted a formation of enemy bombers closing in on the Lexington. They attacked, but the wingman's guns were jammed. O'Hare went from side to side of the V formation of bombers, taking out the outermost one each time. He shot down five bombers in less than four minutes. The remaining enemy planes aborted their bombing run. The Lexington was safe. In 1943, Butch was promoted to Lieutenant Commander and given command of an air group aboard the USS Enterprise.

Lieutenant Eddie O'Hare

On November 26 the Lexington's radar picked up a group of inbound "Bettys",as Japanese bombers were called. Butch's air group was launched. Butch and his wingman, Ensign Andy

Skon, spotted the Bettys flying at wave height closing in on the Lexington. The Bettys were close enough that the Lexington's escorts opened fire with anti-aircraft guns. Despite the rounds exploding around them, they repeatedly attacked the enemy. The Japanese flight group turned away. Butch and Skon gave chase. Two more Hellcats joined them. Now the bomber's escorts surrounded them. One of the escorts got behind Butch and fired a burst from his machine gun. Skon said he saw a white puff of smoke come out of Butch's Hellcat. Because Skon was still in the dogfight, he lost sight of Butch.

On December 9, Butch's family received word that he was MIA. One year later his status was changed to KIA.

The next time you fly into Chicago, take a minute and visit Terminal One. Displayed there, is a fully restored Wildcat and Butch's service medals including a Distinguished Flying Cross with a Gold Star, and a Congressional Medal of Honor. As you leave the airport, turn around and see Chicago's tribute to Butch: "WELCOME TO CHICAGO O'HARE AIRPORT"

Hand Salute----------Ready, Two

WALKER MELVILLE MAHURIN

Walker Melville Mahurin was born on December 5, 1918 in Benton Harbor, Michigan. His family nicknamed him "Bud". This nickname would follow him throughout his life. During his youth, flying and airplanes were just coming into their own. Most young boys wanted to be pilots. With Bud, this dream of flying was strong enough that in 1941, three months before Pearl Harbor, he joined the Army Air Corps.

In January 1943 he was sent to England as part of the 63rd Fighter Squadron to escort Liberator bombers. Before he even saw combat, while still in training, his Thunderbolt was caught up in a Liberator's wake and thrown into its prop. His first "downed" aircraft was his own.

On August 17, while escorting Liberators to Schwein Regensburg, he atoned for the loss of his own aircraft by downing two Focke-Wulf 190s. Just two months later, he racked up three more kills, thus achieving the title "ace". Before the end of the year, that number doubled to ten, making him a "double ace".

Colonel Walker "Bud" Mahurin

On March 27, 1944 his luck ran out. He was attacking a Dornier bomber over northern France. He destroyed the Dornier, but returning fire damaged his P-47. Bud was forced to bail out. The French resistance took him in. It took six weeks, but the underground was able to get him back to England.

Bud had acquired too much knowledge of the French underground to risk another bailout over Europe, and possible capture by the Germans. He was to be sent stateside. He said he didn't know how to fly a desk, and asked to be transferred to the Pacific theater of the war. His request was granted.

Now flying a P-51 Mustang, a Jap bomber was quick work for Bud. He continued downing Japanese planes until war's end. He had totaled over twenty kills. He was a double ace in both theaters of war.

P-51 Mustang

After the war, he remained in the air force. By the outbreak of the Korean Conflict, he had made Lieutenant Colonel, and was flying an F-86 Sabre. By March 5, 1952 he had shot down three MiG-15s. On May 13 his luck ran out again. He was shot down and captured by North Koreans. He spent the next sixteen months being tortured every day as a POW. Upon his release, he was promoted to full colonel before retiring.

America honored him with the Distinguished Service Cross, the Silver Star, and the Distinguished Flying Cross. The British government awarded him with their Distinguished Flying Cross as well.

On May 11, 2010 Walker "Bud" Mahurin passed away.

Hand Salute----------Ready, Two

EDWARD A. CARTER

Edward A. Carter was born in Los Angeles, California on May 26, 1916. He was still an infant when his missionary parents relocated to Shanghai, China. Being educated there, he learned four languages.

At fifteen years of age, he ran away from home and joined the Chinese army. He quickly rose to the rank of Lieutenant. When his superiors learned his true age, he was discharged and returned to his parents.

When he was old enough, he went to Spain and fought in the Spanish Civil War. As a volunteer, he fought against General Franco's fascist troops. In 1938, he was forced to flee to France, which led to his return to the United States.

On September 6, 1941 he joined the U.S. Army. He had learned a lot about the military given his history, and within a year, he was Staff Sergeant Carter. His platoon was being shipped to Europe for combat duties. There was a problem. Sergeant Carter was African-American. He was told that a black non-com could not command white soldiers. He took a "voluntary" demotion to stay with his unit.

In March of 1945, Private Carter's unit was sent to secure bridgeheads near Speyer, Germany. His squad was riding on a tank when they came under heavy enemy fire from machine guns and anti-armor fire from a warehouse. He and three others advanced on the warehouse. 150 yards of open ground had to be covered. As they advanced, one of the four was killed. Carter told the two remaining to give him cover. Carter advanced alone. Of the two providing cover fire, one was killed, and the other was seriously wounded. Carter continued his advance to within thirty yards of the warehouse, and engaged the attackers, knocking out two machine guns and a mortar crew. This was not without cost to him. He received three rounds to his left arm, one round to his left leg, one more to his left hand, and three shrapnel wounds.

Carter's blood-covered body lay motionless on the ground for two hours. Eight Germans from the warehouse slowly approached him. He jumped up with his .45 caliber submachine gun and killed six of them. He took the other two prisoner.

Private Edward Carter

He was recommended for the Medal of Honor, but there was a problem. Although, black men have received the Medal of Honor in every armed conflict of this country since the Civil War, none had been awarded it in World War II. He received a Distinguished Service Cross instead.

With a lingering problem from the shrapnel still in his neck, Private Edward Carter passed away on January 30, 1963. He was laid to rest in the National Cemetery in West Los Angeles.

In 1992, the inequities of the awarding of the Medal of Honor during World War II were corrected. Staff Sergeant Edward Carter was one of the many to be raised to that honor. His remains were exhumed. He now rests in Arlington, Virginia.

Hand Salute----------Ready, Two

TIBOR RUBIN

It's hard to imagine the hardships that lay ahead in life for a Jew born in Hungary in 1929. On June 18, Tibor Rubin came into such a life.

Tibor was just 13 years old when the Nazis separated him from his family. He was sent to the Mauthausen Concentration Camp. It would be years later that he learned his parents, and two sisters, had died in the Auschwitz gas chamber. This young child survived alone for fourteen months before American soldiers liberated him and the rest of the camp. "We were filthy and stunk. Disease was everywhere. The American soldiers had compassion for all of us." It was then that Tibor vowed he would one day become an American soldier.

Tibor was still in his teens when he immigrated to the US. He tried twice to join the army, but was told both times that his English was below standard. He took classes and worked hard, and the third time was the charm.

By July 1950 Corporal Tibor Rubin was in the Republic of Korea with the 8th Cavalry Regiment. During the battle for control of the Pusan Perimeter, his company was overwhelmed by thousands of enemy troops. Tibor jumped behind the only remaining machine gun, inflicting countless enemy casualties. He stayed behind his withdrawing company delaying the advancing enemy and allowing his company's safe withdrawal.

During the Battle of Unsan, again the enemy overran his company. This time, Tibor was wounded with shrapnel in the hand and chest. He and many others were taken prisoner. They were taken on a long, forced march to a POW camp. Those who lagged behind were shot. While at the camp, prisoners were dying at thirty to forty a day from starvation and untreated wounds. Tibor discovered he was able to "escape" at night and reach enemy supplies. He then returned to the camp with food and medical supplies. Getting caught meant getting shot. He continued his almost nightly escapes for two and a half years before American soldiers again liberated him. He is credited with saving over forty lives.

Corporal Tibor Rubin

It took over fifty years to recognize this hero, but on September 23, 2005 President George Bush draped a Medal of Honor around Tibor's neck. The citation states in part, "serving in the highest tradition." Tibor Rubin has truly fulfilled the vow he made that day at Mauthausen.

Hand Salute----------Ready, Two

EILEEN NEARNE

On September 1, 2010 the body of an 89-year-old indigent woman was found in a small apartment in Torquay, England. She was destined for a pauper's grave until a routine police check uncovered an amazing past history.

Eileen Nearne was raised in France, so French was her first language. In the mid-thirties, her parents, fearing the rise of Adolf Hitler, immigrated to England.

In the early years of World War II, Eileen was one of thirty-nine British women that parachuted into German-occupied France. Her job was to make contact with the French resistance, then set up a covert radio link between them and London. The object was to coordinate individual groups of resistance into organized attacks on the Germans. She also arranged drop zones for the British to parachute arms to supply the resistance. Eileen parachuted into an area near Paris. It took her several days to make contact with a member of the resistance, but before too long her radio station was up and running.

While operating her radio station, on two occasions, she narrowly escaped capture by the Gestapo, but in July 1944 she was captured and sent to Ravensbruck Concentration Camp near Berlin. She was twenty-three years old. She was stripped naked and beaten daily. She was submerged in ice water, but stuck to her cover story.

She was just a gullible local girl transmitting coded messages she didn't understand. She was moved to Archipelago, a death camp where her head was shaved. Still she didn't reveal any resistance names or information. In December of 1944, she was again moved to Markleberg, a forced labor camp. While in Markleberg, she and two other women were able to escape. They made their way south, and finally made contact with American troops. Eileen was returned to England, but was still not home free.

Back in England, American intelligence officers initially identified her as a Nazi collaborator. She was held in a detention camp surrounded by captured SS personnel until her account of aiding the British could be verified.

Eileen Nearne

That pauper's grave was denied this one.

Eileen Nearne was laid to rest with full military honors, with a military honor guard, and dignitaries from both England and France in attendance. Her coffin was topped with a red satin pillow to which were fastened her military medals, including a Croix de Guerre awarded to her by the French government.

Hand Salute----------Ready, Two

STUBBY

It is the responsibility of the Quartermaster Corps to maintain all K9 units that support our military personnel. All military dogs are inducted, trained, assigned, deployed, discharged, and unfortunately sometimes interred by the Quartermaster Corps. They guard, sniff explosives, serve with the military police, scout, detect mines, and many other duties. But where did it all begin?

Corporal J. Robert Conroy was training at Yale Bowl, Connecticut in the summer of 1917 when a scruffy stray pit bull approached him. "Stubby", as he would become known, was smart. Conroy even taught Stubby to salute on command. When Conroy boarded the S.S. Minnesota headed for France, he had Stubby under his jacket.

On their first night in the trenches, Stubby noticed that when the soldiers heard the whine of an incoming rocket, they dove for cover. A frightening explosion followed. After that, because of his sensitive hearing, he was able to warn the soldiers of incoming by taking cover before the soldiers heard the whine. The men followed his lead.

Conroy's unit was involved in seventeen battles. One night, as the exhausted men were sleeping, the Germans placed a chlorine gas bomb upwind of Conroy's unit. Stubby noticed the offensive odor and barked to arouse the men. They all donned their gas masks and were saved, but there wasn't a gas mask that would fit their four-legged hero. Stubby went down. Conroy carried him to an aid station, and stayed with him through the night. Stubby survived.

After the armistice, Stubby returned to the states with his unit. When his actions became known, he became our first K9 hero. Congress even had special medals minted for him. He was made an honorary lifetime member of the Red Cross and the American Legion.

"Stubby"

After the excitement of his heroic deeds died down, Stubby went into semi-retirement as the mascot of Georgetown University's football team.

Dogs have served in every armed conflict America has had since Stubby's usefulness was recognized. It is estimated that in Vietnam alone, dogs were responsible for saving 10,000 American lives.

For Stubby and the rest of the K9 heroes that are too often overlooked.

Hand Salute----------Ready, Two

SALVATORE GIUNTA

On the night of October 25, 2007 Sergeant Joshua Brennan was in a field hospital in eastern Afghanistan, awaiting surgery due to wounds inflicted by Taliban fighters earlier that night. Even in his wounded condition, he was able to begin writing his recommendation regarding the heroic actions of Sergeant Salvatore Giunta. Sergeant Brennan was unable to finish his recommendation. He died in that surgery. Other members of his unit did finish it. The recommendation started its way up through the chain of command.

It had just gotten dark on the 25th, when Sergeant Brennan led his unit into the Korengal Valley, nicknamed the "Valley of Death" by American soldiers. The nickname was a result of forty-two American soldiers being killed there before they abandoned their outpost in the valley in April 2010. Their mission that night was to recover US equipment abandoned after a firefight two days earlier.

Because they had been monitoring Taliban communications, the men were aware that the enemy wanted to capture a live soldier as a trophy. Suddenly, the unit was attacked. The man in front of Sergeant Ginunta had been knocked unconscious from a round that struck his helmet. While dragging the man to a place of cover, Ginunta took two rounds to the chest, but was saved by his body armor. He saw that Specialist Frank Eckrode had been downed, shot four times.

While under heavy fire, Ginunta tended to Eckrode's wounds, then he saw Sergeant Brennan had been wounded, and was being carried off by two Taliban fighters. Ginunta fired once, killing one of the two. He fired several more rounds wounding the other. Ginunta tended to the Sergeant's wounds and guarded over him for a half hour until a medevac helicopter could evacuate him.

Salvatore Giunta

Since Vietnam, there have been only nine service members to be honored with our nation's highest award. All of which were awarded posthumously. On November 16, 2010 a Medal of Honor was draped around the neck of Staff Sergeant Salvatore Giunta. The Sergeant's response, "I'm just a mediocre soldier. I was just doing my job."

He was the first surviving recipient of that honor since Vietnam.

Hand Salute----------Ready, Two

CHANNING MOSS

The RPG is commonly known in the western world as a rocket-propelled grenade. However, the actual name of this Soviet-made weapon is a Ruchnoy Protivotankovyy Granatomyot, meaning, hand held anti-tank grenade launcher. The most common used by insurgents in Afghanistan is the RPG-7. The RPG-7 has several types of warheads. Some detonate upon impact. Some detonate a preset time after impact.

RPG-7

On March 16, 2006 in southeastern Afghanistan, a group of five Humvees were patrolling along the Pakistan border. Private Channing Moss was a gunner and was positioned atop of one of them. Suddenly, insurgents attacked their small convoy.

An RPG smashed through the windshield of Moss's Humvee. The round struck Moss in his right hip. It didn't detonate, yet. The baseball-bat sized bomb was lodged inside him. The only medic for many miles just happened to be riding in the same Humvee. It was Moss's best friend, Jared Angel. Army protocol and common sense dictates to keep away from unexploded rounds. Jared stayed with his friend and treated him. Jared then stabilized the round against movement, which could cause detonation. An evac helicopter was called. When it landed, the pilot disregarded his own safety, and knowingly loaded Moss onboard, including the unexploded ordinance. Moss was flown to the army hospital in Pashtun Province where a group of army doctors again violated policy by taking this human bomb into the operating room. Dr. John Oh, a

Korean immigrant and West Point graduate, along with several volunteers, and an explosive disposal team, successfully removed the round from Moss's body. Moss survived. Private Channing Moss has had six subsequent surgeries and will require lifelong medical care, but he is doing well back home in Gainesville, Georgia.

This is for all the "common, ordinary G.I.s" who disregarded army protocol, common sense, and their own safety.

Hand Salute----------Ready, Two

HERSHEL WILLIAMS

The island is only two miles wide by four miles long. The name *Iwo Jima* in Japanese means, "Sulfur Island." It's made up of barren volcanic rock and sand, but the existence of an airfield on this tiny island would put the Japanese homeland within range of our bombers. We needed this Japanese-held island.

Several days of heavy bombardment by naval guns and air corps bombers did little to reduce the resistance by the enemy. Because the enemy was not on the island, they were *in* the island. Years of Japanese occupation had allowed them to dig a massive underground network of over 800 concrete pillboxes each armed with a machine gun, and over eleven miles of tunnels connecting them together.

Corporal Hershel W. "Woody" Williams was part of the second wave to hit the beach. Woody had seen combat on Guam and thought it was rough. It would prove to be a "walk in the park" when compared with Iwo Jima. He was armed with a flamethrower, which proved to be more effective against the subterranean pillboxes than small arms fire. This seventy-pound weapon is like a giant squirt gun that shoots a stream of ignited jellied gasoline.

Woody's unit was being held down by several of the concrete protected machine guns. American tanks were unable to move in the volcanic sand and would not be of help. Covered by four riflemen, Woody crawled forward until he was in range of the first pillbox. A blast from his flamethrower silenced it. He spent the next four hours taking out one pillbox after another. He retreated only long enough to retrieve filled tanks for his weapon. At one point he found himself on top of a pillbox. He located the air vent protruding just above ground. Placing the nozzle of the flamethrower into the vent, he fired. The machine gun was silenced. Those four hours were all while under heavy enemy fire.

The fighting for this eight square mile island was so intense that the demand for actions "above and beyond" was behind every rock. This thirty-six day battle yielded twenty-seven Medals of Honor, our nation's highest medal for valor. This is one third of the eighty-two Medals of Honor earned during all of World War II.

Corporal Hershel "Woody" Williams

On October 5, 1945 President Harry S. Truman draped a Medal of Honor around the neck of Corporal Hershel W. Williams.

Hand Salute----------Ready, Two

GUY LOUIS GABALDON

Halfway between Australia and Japan is a group of 15 islands called the Marianas. The northernmost of the Marianas is the largest island of the chain, at a little over forty-four square miles and named Saipan.

In June of 1944, the Japanese were no longer in control of the Pacific and were fighting a defensive war, but Saipan was still under their control as it had been for many years. With Japan only 1300 miles north, it would put the Japanese homeland within range of our B-29 bombers. We wanted this island.

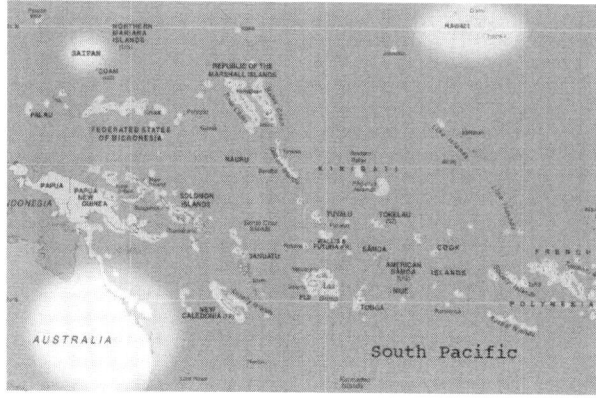

Saipan

On March 22, 1926 Guy Louis Gabaldon was born into a large family of Mexican-decent in the ghetto of East Los Angeles. With poverty and the threat of gang violence so prominent in his youth, at age twelve, he left home and moved in with his extended family, the Nanaios. The Nanaios were of Japanese descent. During the remainder of his youth, he learned to speak Japanese. At the outbreak of World War II, the Nanaios were placed in an internment camp. Guy joined the marine corps.

On June 15, 1944 Private First Class Guy Gabaldon was among the 8000 marines to land on the West coast of Saipan. The estimated 29,000 Japanese on the island knew they would lose the island, but their orders were to kill as many Americans as they could before sacrificing their own life for the honor of their Emperor. This resulted in many massive "banzai" attacks. The Japanese had also convinced the island natives that if the Americans captured them, they would suffer unspeakable torture. This resulted in mass suicides, most by leaping off cliffs onto the rocky shore. The marines began referring to the island as "Suicide Island".

On the first night on the island, Gabaldon snuck away from his unit and crawled behind enemy lines. He crawled into Japanese caves. He was able to talk to the enemy soldiers in their own language promising fair treatment and hot food if they surrendered, and also that they would be returned to Japan after the war ended. He spent the entire night going from tunnel to tunnel. As morning approached, he returned to his unit with fifty Japanese POWs.

Instead of a hero's welcome, his commanding officer advised Gabaldon that he would be court-martialed for his unauthorized mission. Despite this, Gabaldon continued his nightly "raids" until his fellow marines nicknamed him "The Pied Piper of Saipan". By July 9, the Americans had gained control of the island. The Pied Piper had taken over 1000 Japanese POWs without a single shot. This meant that there were 1000 Japanese that were *not* shooting at American marines. The pending court-martial was dropped. Instead, the Pied Piper was recommended for the Silver Star. This recommendation was upgraded and Private First Class Guy Louis Gabaldon was awarded the Navy Cross.

On August 31, 2006 The Pied Piper of Saipan passed away. He is now at peace in Arlington National Cemetery.

Hand Salute----------Ready, Two

DR. LAWTON E. SHANK

"December 7, 1941 a date which will live in infamy." Although a relatively small portion of Americans were directly involved, virtually the entire world would suffer the aftermath.

The Marshall Islands are southwest of Pearl Harbor, halfway to Australia. The northernmost one of the islands is called Wake Island.

On December 6, the entire military population of Wake consisted of 449 marines, 68 navy personnel, and 5 army soldiers. There were also 1150 civilians on the island employed by the Morrison-Knudsen Corporation out of Boise, Idaho. The civilians were building a seaplane base.

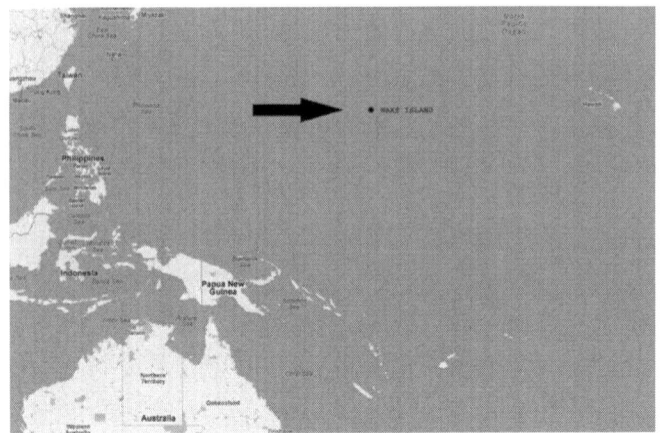

Wake Island

On December 8, a group of Japanese bombers and fighters attacked Wake Island. Dr. Lawton E. Shank, a civilian, treated the wounded throughout the battle, even as the hospital was falling around him. He organized the moving of the wounded, and some of the equipment, into an empty storage container and continued to treat the wounded.

At first, the enemy was forced to withdraw, but the battle continued for twenty-four days. On December the 23, the island fell to the Japanese. Twenty-three marines and ten civilians had lost their lives. The remaining Americans were taken prisoner. Most were shipped out to China and Japan, but a group including Dr. Shank was kept on the island to be used as forced labor. The prisoners were beaten and tortured daily. Dr. Shank was credited with keeping the Americans alive during their nearly two-year captivity.

By October 1943, American forces were taking back the Pacific. It became obvious that Wake would soon fall back into American hands. On October 7, the remaining ninety-eight prisoners, including Dr. Shank, were blindfolded and forced to sit on the edge of a deep trench. Japanese machine guns mowed them down. They were buried where they fell. It was suspected that one of the Americans had escaped. The dead were dug up and counted. Ninety-seven. The last man was found, beheaded, and buried with the others.

Dr. Lawton E. Shank was recommended for the Medal of Honor, but due to his civilian status, it was downgraded to a Navy Cross, and presented posthumously. This is the only Navy Cross ever presented to a civilian.

Hand Salute----------Ready, Two

ROBERT LEWIS HOWARD

Robert Lewis Howard came into this world on July 11, 1939 in Opelika, Alabama. Growing up, he deeply admired his father and uncle. Both were air born soldiers and served in Europe during World War II. This might have been the start of his devotion and service to America. No one around him was surprised when, in 1956 at age seventeen, he enlisted in the army. Maybe it was his admiration for his father and uncle that drove him.

By the time Vietnam heated up, now Staff Sergeant Howard had earned his wings as a Green Beret. He was a member of a highly classified Military Assistance Command. His unit was on a covert mission deep inside Laos to rescue a downed American pilot. During that mission he demonstrated actions "above and beyond" and was recommended to receive the Medal of Honor. However, because "there were no American troops in Laos", military command was afraid of the publicity surrounding a Medal of Honor recipient, and downgraded the recommendation to a Silver Star, promoting him to Master Sergeant.

On another top-secret mission in Laos, again he demonstrated he had what it takes, and was recommended for the Medal of Honor a second time. Remember, we supposedly had no American troops in Laos. Again it was downgraded. This time he received a Distinguished Service Cross. He was also commissioned as a First Lieutenant.

Now, an officer of a mixed unit of American and South Vietnamese, he was deep inside North Vietnamese-held territory when two companies of Viet Cong surrounded their unit. During the initial engagement, Lieutenant Howard was wounded, and his weapon destroyed, by an enemy grenade. He saw that his platoon leader had been wounded seriously and was exposed to enemy fire. Lieutenant Howard crawled through a hail of enemy fire to his fallen leader. As he was administrating first aid, a round struck his ammo pouch exploding several magazines wounding him further. He dragged his wounded leader through heavy enemy fire back to the platoon's location. He reorganized the platoon and began a defensive action. It took three and a half hours, but they were able to gain sufficient control to allow evac helicopters to land. Though badly wounded himself, he carried wounded to the helicopters, and was the last to board. On March 2, 1971 President Richard Nixon draped the Medal of Honor around the neck of First Lieutenant Robert Howard.

After serving forty-six years in the army, fifty-four months of which were in combat, resulting in his being wounded fourteen times, on September 29, 1992 now full Colonel Robert Howard, retired. At that time, he had acquired the Medal of Honor, two Distinguished Service Crosses, a Silver Star, four Bronze Stars, four Legion of Merits with three oak leaf clusters, and eight Purple Hearts.

Colonel Robert Howard

On December 23, 2009 Colonel Robert Howard passed away. He now rests in Arlington National Cemetery.

Hand Salute----------Ready, Two

HARVEY BARNUM

In 1958, the senior class at Cheshire High School in Connecticut held an assembly to hear recruiting officers of four military service branches speak. The first three each spoke, attempting to sell their branch as the best to consider joining. Throughout their talks, the seniors were talking, catcalling, and generally disruptive. The marine recruiter got up and said that the class was rude and immature, and there was no one there that was good enough to be in his marine corps. Then he sat back down. One senior, Harvey Barnum, said to himself, "I'm going to prove him wrong."

After graduation, Harvey joined the Marine Corps Reserve. He served there while earning a Bachelor of Arts in Economics. He accepted a commission and appointment in the regular Marine Corps and served as a forward observer. In December of 1964, he was promoted to First

Lieutenant. In December 1965, Lieutenant Barnum was deployed to Vietnam.

His company was suddenly attacked and surrounded. A hail of extremely accurate enemy fire pinned down the entire company. They were more than 500 meters of open and fire-swept ground away, from any semblance of a safe area, and casualties mounted rapidly. Lieutenant Barnum quickly looked around seeking targets for his artillery. He found the radio operator who had been killed, and the company commander who was mortally wounded. He gave aid to the dying commander then he took the radio from the dead marine. Lieutenant Barnum assumed command of the rifle company. He reorganized the company and replaced the lost key personnel with riflemen. To better view enemy positions, he stood up amidst the heavy enemy fire, and began transmitting targets for his artillery batteries. They were able to clear enough ground to enable two evac helicopters to land to remove the dead and wounded. He led the remainder of the company and they were able to take out their original objective.

For this action, he was decorated with the Medal of Honor.

By the time his tour in Vietnam was finished, he had made the rank of Captain. He returned to Vietnam in October of 1968 for a second tour. In October of 1969, he was promoted to Major. By the time that tour was over, he had earned a Bronze Star with a combat "V", and a Gold Star, the Navy Achievement Medal with a combat "V", the

Vietnamese Gallantry Cross with Silver Star, and a Purple Heart.

In May of 1972, he was promoted to Lieutenant Colonel.

Colonel Harvey Barnum

In August of 1989, after serving twenty-seven years as a marine, now full Colonel Harvey Barnum, retired. He had proven the recruiting officer wrong.

Hand Salute----------Ready, Two

MATT URBAN

Shortly after the end of World War I, Stanley and Helen Urbanowitz left Poland and immigrated to America. They settled in Buffalo, New York where Helen gave birth to a son, Matty Louis. Matty's father, Stanley, wanting to be as American as he could, changed the family name to Urban.

After Matt Urban graduated Buffalo East High School, he attended Cornell University in Ithaca, New York where he was a member of the ROTC while he earned a degree in history and government. After graduation, the ROTC involvement earned him a commission in the U.S. Army. By the end of 1941, he was fighting the Germans in France.

In early 1944, now Captain Urban was a company commander in the 9th Infantry Division. On June 14 of that year, his company was engaged by Germans with heavy small-arms fire, and two Panzer tanks near Renouf, France. The tanks were unmercifully raking Urban's company and inflicting heavy casualties. He armed himself with a 3.5-inch rocket launcher, called a bazooka, and along with an ammo carrier, made it to a place near the tanks.

Under heavy fire, he stood up to discharge the rockets, and he destroyed both tanks. Though he had been wounded by a 37mm tank gun, he refused evacuation and continued leading his company. An hour later he was wounded two more times. One of the injuries was serious, and he was evacuated. His wounds were not yet healed when, against doctor's orders, he left the hospital and hitchhiked back to his unit near St. Lô, France. He located his company; they were being held up by strong enemy fire. His unit had a supporting tank, but the crew had been killed. He found a lieutenant that thought he could drive it. Captain Urban mounted the machine gun and they pushed forward, destroying the enemy. This time the Captain was wounded in the chest, but again refused evacuation. This was not to be the last of his combat wounds.

The citation reads in part, "...distinguished himself by a series of heroic actions from 14 June to 3 September, 1944, in at least 5 separate battles, in France and Belgium..." Before the war ended, he had earned the Medal of Honor, plus the Legion of Merit, three Bronze Stars with "V", seven Purple Hearts, the French Croix De Guerre with Silver Gilt Star and Palm, the Belgium Croix de Guerre Palm, and the Belgium Forragere.

He attained the rank of Lieutenant Colonel before February 26, 1946 when he was forced to retire because of his combat wounds. He spent the next four decades serving in community and veteran organizations.

Lieutenant Colonel Matt Urban

On March 4, 1995 Matt Urban, (Matty Louis Urbanowitz) passed away. He now rests in Arlington National Cemetery

Hand Salute----------Ready, Two

ROLAND WOLFE

In 1938, it was clear to those in power in England that war with Germany was inevitable. In order to be prepared, they began mass production of a single seat fighter called a Spitfire.

It would prove to be a formidable adversary against the Luftwaffe's Messerschmitt Bf109. The Spitfire, with its 1175 hp Rolls Royce engine, was capable of 362 mph, with a range of over 434 miles. It was armed with eight .303 machine guns, and a 20mm nose cannon. On September 3, 1939 the inevitable began. England's new problem; more Spitfires than qualified pilots.

Spitfire

A large number of qualified pilots were recruited from America, but since America was not at war with Germany at the time, these men were stripped of their American citizenship. Among these men was Roland "Bud" Wolfe. Bud Wolfe was born in 1917 in Nebraska. He grew up with a passion for flying. He was well qualified and knew that England's war was a *just* war, so he joined the Royal Air Force, or RAF.

Roland "Bud" Wolfe

The 133 Squadron, known as the Eagle Squadron, was based at the northern tip of England and was made up of all Americans. Their job was to fly "top cover" to protect inbound convoys from U-boat attacks as far out over the Atlantic as their Spitfire's range would allow.

On November 30, 1941 Bud was returning to his home base when his Rolls Royce engine overheated and seized up. He parachuted to safety, while his Spitfire pancaked into a bog just seven miles from England, inside Ireland. A bog is a marsh, and is not unlike quicksand. The Spitfire sank from view.

Ireland was a neutral country and had decided that any warring military personal would be held in a POW camp for the duration. Bud was interred at Curragh POW camp along with English and German Prisoners. The prisoners were treated well, but Bud refused to sit out the war with the enemy. One night he was able to escape and made it back to his home base.

The English government, for political reasons, returned him to Ireland and the POW camp. He made several more escape attempts, but failed. He remained a POW until 1943 when Carragh Camp was closed and the prisoners were returned to their home countries. Bud was able to get his citizenship reinstated, and he joined the army air corps. He spent the remainder of the war flying missions over Europe. In 1950, Bud was still in what was then the Air Force, and flew against North Korea. He wasn't done yet. He also fought in the Vietnam War.

On June 29, 2011 his Spitfire was recovered from the bog in Ireland, but Bud wasn't there to see it. He had passed away in 1994.

Roland "Bud" Wolfe never returned to America with a chest covered with medals. He never had a ticker-tape parade, or other suitable recognition, but this was a real American hero.

Hand Salute----------Ready, Two

CARL LUCAS NORDEN

During World War II, the Third Reich had many closely guarded secrets. Arguably, at the top of that list was their Enigma machine, a device that enabled the high command to communicate confidential information with their military command. Early in 1944, unbeknownst to the Germans, the allies captured one of these machines. Through reverse engineering, they were able to duplicate it. From then on, the allies were able to decipher German communications, which saved countless lives and shortened the war.

We also had our closely guarded secrets.

Carl Lucas Norden was born April 23, 1880 in Semarang, Java, which is now Indonesia. His family soon returned to their native Holland, and then made another move to Dresden, Germany. In 1896, he began a three-year apprenticeship in a Swiss machine shop, while he earned a degree in mechanical engineering.

In 1904 Carl immigrated to the United States, and worked in a machine shop in Brooklyn. In the next few years, Carl won several patents for such things as a pilotless target plane, a catapult launching-device to launch aircraft from aircraft carriers, and a control system for aircraft, which was a precursor to the autopilot. Perhaps the most important instrument he developed was the Norden bombsight. This instrument was a very early form of a computer. It calculated airspeed, groundspeed, wind, altitude, and the speed of a falling bomb.

As the bomber approached the target, the pilot turned control of the aircraft over to the bombardier. The bombsight told the bombardier the precise second to release the payload. From 12,000 to 15,000 feet the bombs could hit within 164 feet of the target. It made daytime precision bombing possible. Even the Enola Gay used this sight over Hiroshima.

Norden Bombsight

This bombsight was so important that it was at the top of our top-secret list. The sight was loaded onto the aircraft just before a mission, and then removed upon returning. The bombardier had orders to destroy the sight in the event the plane was going down, even at the cost of his life. The existence of the sight was well known, but how it worked was kept secret until after the war. Carl Norden sold the rights to the sight to the United States government for $1.00.

After the war ended, he moved back to Switzerland where he passed away in 1965.

Carl Lucas Norden never wore a uniform. Not all of our heroes did.

Hand Salute----------Ready, Two

NANCY WAKE

Nancy Wake was born August 30, 1912 in Wellington, New Zealand, the youngest of six children. Two years later her family moved to Sidney, Australia. In 1916, her father abandoned the family leaving her mother to raise the six children. Nancy learned to be a survivor. While still very young, she left home to work as a nurse.

She received a small amount of money from an aunt. It was enough for her to go to England, then on to France, where she worked as a freelance journalist for the Hearst newspaper group. Among her assignments was an interview with Hitler in 1933. Nancy knew then that this man would be a problem. She didn't know how big of a problem, or how he would change her life. While on an assignment in Vienna, she witnessed the persecution of Jews and other minorities.

She returned to France and married industrialist Henri Fiocca. They settled in Marseilles. War broke out, and as it heated up Nancy began smuggling refugees and downed allied pilots into Spain. Soon, the number she had saved was in the hundreds. She became too well known and the Gestapo learned her name, but she continued to elude capture. A price of five million francs was put on her head. She was so good at eluding capture the Gestapo nicknamed her, "The White Mouse." It wasn't long before she was number one on the Gestapo's most wanted list. She escalated her involvement in the resistances. Before too long she was forced to flee through Spain to England, leaving her husband, friends, and life behind.

In order to be better at what she had been doing, she joined the French section of the British Special Operations Executive, and received intense guerilla fighting training. On April 29, 1944 she returned to France by parachute at night. She received airdrops of weapons and explosives. She organized groups of resistance fighters. They destroyed German supply depots and interrupted their supply lines. All this was in preparation for D-day.

Nancy continued her efforts until the Germans were forced out of France. One of her comrades in the resistance, Henri Tardivat, later described her as, "the most feminine women I know, until the fighting starts. Then she is like five men."

Nancy Wake

Several European governments recognized her fight against the Germans. She received the George Medal from Britain, the Medaille De La Résistance, Chevaliers d'Honneur, three Croix De Guerre - two with bronze palms and one with a silver star from France, and the Medal of Freedom with a bronze palm from the United States.

It was several years after the war ended, that Nancy learned that her husband, Henri Fiocca had been tortured and murdered by the Gestapo because he refused to give up The White Mouse.

On August 8, 2011 Nancy Wake Fiocca, The White Mouse passed away.

Hand Salute----------Ready, Two

DR. ALBERT BROWN

Albert Brown was born in North Platte, Nebraska. In 1905, he earned a Doctor of Dental Surgery degree at Creighton University. He had built a successful dentistry practice over the next decade when he was called to serve in the marines. He left his wife, Helen, his young son and daughter, and his practice, to serve his country.

Shortly after the US entered the war in the Pacific, the Japanese made a major push to take control of the Philippines. Their push started on the Bataan Peninsula. Unfortunately for Albert "Doc" Brown, this was his first assignment as a marine. The Filipinos fought side by side with US Marines. It took three months of intense combat, but by April of 1942, the Japanese took control of the Peninsula. There were 22,000 marines and 50,000 civilians taken prisoner.

On April 7, the Japanese commander, General Homma, gave the order to march the prisoners, including Doc Brown, seventy miles north to Camp O'Donnell, a former US military base, now a POW camp. They were given three days to accomplish this. Any prisoner that fell down was shot or bayoneted. As trucks of Japanese soldiers passed the columns of prisoners, bayonets were hung out of the side, and prisoners were decapitated just for fun. They were denied food or water. The march lasted seven days.

It's estimated that 18,000 to 20,000 prisoners died en route. The rest of the prisoners remained in the POW camp at forced labor until September of 1945. They died at an estimated rate of fifteen to twenty a day. After Japan surrendered, the camp was liberated. General Homma was convicted of war crimes and executed.

The now nearly blind, 80-pound Doc Brown spent the next two years in the hospital, suffering from a broken back, a broken neck, malaria, dysentery, and dengue fever. He eventually made it home, but was physically unable to resume his dental practice.

Infamous Bataan Death March

In 2007, Albert Doc Brown was recognized as the last survivor of the infamous Bataan Death March. He said that when he was taken prisoner, he was almost 40 years old.

Men much younger and stronger were dying all around him, yet he survived. On August 14, 2011 Doc Brown passed away at 105 years of age.

This is for Doc Brown and the other 72,000 taken prisoner in April of 1943.

Hand Salute----------Ready, Two

GEORGE EDWARD HUNT

During World War II, the submarine was an indispensable weapon for both sides. While on the surface, its firepower is limited. However, while submerged, its torpedoes can be devastating to the enemy. Due to the sheer size of the ammunition, which varies from 14 to 20 feet long, the average submarine could only carry twenty-four torpedoes. Obviously, accuracy was critical. Everybody is well aware of the effectiveness of the wolf packs of German U-boats in the North Atlantic. Submarines were also an effective tool for the Japanese in the Pacific Theater. Of course, America used their underwater fleet extensively. This effective weapon is well documented in the news, books, and movies. But, not a great deal has been said about allies that also used this weapon. The British Royal Navy had a small, but very effective fleet of submarines.

Captain George Edward Hunt

George Edward Hunt was born on July 4, 1916 in Glasgow, Scotland. He was educated at St. Ninian's, and cared for by two doting aunts. At age 13, he left and joined the Merchant Navy training ship, HMS Conway. At sixteen, he joined the Henderson line, which sailed between India and Burma.

In 1930, he was commissioned as a Midshipman RNR, and in 1938, he was transferred to the Royal Navy. After a year of tactical courses, he then went on board the destroyer Foxhound, before volunteering for submarine service. On board his first submarine, he served as the signals and navigation officer.

On April 29, 1940 in a dense fog, his sub was hit and cut into by a Norwegian merchant ship. Hunt was instrumental in getting all but two crewmembers out, and then keeping them together until they were rescued. He was awarded a Distinguished Service Cross.

In June of that year, he was assigned as liaison officer to the Dutch submarine, O 10, patrolling the North Sea. They helped evacuate the beaches after the battle of Dunkirk. From December to March of 1941, he was liaison officer on the Polish submarine, Sokol. He was promoted to First Lieutenant and assigned to the submarine, Proteus, in the Mediterranean Sea. The Italian anti-sub ship, Sagittario, attacked the Proteus.

The Proteus lost her forward hydroplane and water poured into the torpedo room. Hunt's leadership proved crucial in keeping the Proteus from sinking. They were able to limp back to home port at periscope depth. For his actions in saving the Proteus, Lieutenant Hunt was awarded a Bar to his Distinguished Service Cross, and promoted.

In April of 1942, Hunt passed the commanding officers 'perisher' course and took command of the submarine, HMS Ultor. The Ultor was sent on patrol in the Mediterranean. Service on the Ultor would forge his reputation.

In April of 1943 the Ultor fired on and sank the German vessel, Penerf. The sinking of two Italian ships soon followed this. In August they sank the Italian destroyer, Lince. On June 27, 1944 he managed to sink the cargo ship Blanc, despite her four escorts. He was hunted for an hour, but slowly drew away. One hour later, he spotted the 5260 ton tanker, Palles under tow by two tugs. Five escorts and four aircraft escorted the Palles. Hunt fired his last two torpedoes. Both hit and the Palles went down. Hunt took the Ultor to the bottom at 300 feet, the maximum safe depth for that submarine, and sat still. Hunt counted the depth charges. After 100, he stopped counting. The enemy finally gave up and left. The Ultor had sustained major damage, but nothing that wasn't manageable. By the end of the war, Hunt held the title of the deadliest submarine captain. He had fired sixty-eight torpedoes with forty-seven percent hitting their target.

Hunt remained in the Royal Navy until he retired, then he immigrated to Australia. He remained there until August 16, 2011 when submarine commander George Hunt passed away.

Hand Salute----------Ready, Two

MARGY REED

Margy Reed was born on August 27, 1916 in Butte, Montana. The location was insignificant, because her parents, Peter Reed and Maybelle Hooper were members of a travelling vaudeville troupe, and Butte was just a stopover. By the age of three, her parents had included Margy in their vaudeville act. Margy was dancing, singing, and acting out parts in comedy skits.

Everybody agreed she had real talent in this field. As she grew up, she developed a love of helping the sick and injured. She started taking nursing classes. Her entertainment career was picking up. In 1934, she made her film debut in a little known short called *A Nite in the Nite Club*. She changed her name, and became Martha Raye.

Martha Raye

Over the next few years, she acted in many movies alongside numerous big names including; Al Jolson, Joe E. Brown, Bob Hope, and W. C. Fields. During this rise in her entertainment career, she continued her nursing classes, and earned an R.N. degree, as a registered nurse. She often volunteered at veteran's hospitals.

After the outbreak of World War II, she began volunteering at the United Service Organization, better known as the USO. This wasn't enough for her. She joined the army reserves. Because of her R.N. status, she was commissioned as a Second Lieutenant.

On May 6, 1941 Martha Raye joined Bob Hope on his first tour to entertain our fighting troops. She was inspired, and joined him on each of his subsequent tours. Martha was a proud American army officer, and would wear her uniform on these tours.

The next decade saw her entertainment career skyrocket. She retained her avocation of nursing by remaining in the army reserves. Her entertainment career was rewarded by many prestigious awards including two stars on Hollywood's Walk of Fame. Her avocation of nursing was rewarded with several promotions.

She continued entertaining the troops with Bob Hope through the Korean Conflict. Now, Colonel Raye continued into Vietnam.

It was just before Thanksgiving 1967. Martha Raye was on one of her tours, west of Pieku, Vietnam when the camp came under heavy enemy fire. A CH-47 Chinook helicopter was called in to evacuate the tour celebrities. It landed and the pilot observed Martha Raye in jungle fatigues loading dead and wounded into the rear. She tended the wounded on the short flight to the field hospital. As the Chinook was being unloaded, a Captain approached Martha, and told her he had immediate transportation for her to a safe location.

Martha said, "Captain, I have a bird on this collar, and a caduceus on this collar which means I'm a nurse. They need me here."

She assisted in the field hospital the rest of the day, and into the night.

She had made over thirty movies and fifteen television shows, but on October 19, 1994 Margy Reed, known to the world as Martha Raye, passed away. She was honored once more by the fulfillment of her last request of being buried with full military honors at Fort Brag, North Carolina. She is the only woman buried there.

Hand Salute----------Ready, Two

Reckless

In 1952, Kim Huk Moon, a young Korean boy in Soule, was selling his horse to raise money to get his sister a prosthetic leg to replace the leg she lost in the conflict with the north. In October, Marine Lieutenant Eric Pedersen was looking for a mascot for his unit, and bought the horse for $250. The antics of the horse, coupled with her insatiable appetite to steal anything edible, endeared her to the men in Pedersen's unit. The men made her an honorary marine and called her "Reckless". Private Reckless began her military career. Not only was she a benefit to the morale of the unit, but also she was useful with the transporting of heavy equipment in the mountainous area where vehicles couldn't travel.

In March of 1953, the most ferocious battle in Marine Corps history took place at Outpost Vegas. The incoming artillery rounds fell at 500 an hour. Lieutenant Pedersen's unit was on the front line.

Private Reckless had been left at the supply dump, to the rear. The marines at the front line were low on ammunition. At the supply dump, they loaded 386 pounds of ammo onto Private Reckless, and slapped her hindquarters.

She took off for the frontline. She ran full speed across "no man's land" and delivered the goods. Two wounded marines were put onto the horse, and she returned to the rear. She was again loaded down with ammo and again, she returned to the front line. She took out more wounded. On one of her trips, she passed three marines unable to return to the main line due to heavy incoming fire.

Moving alongside of Reckless, using her as a shield, they were able to rejoin their unit. Over the course of the five-day battle, she made fifty-one runs up and down the hill, amazingly without anyone leading her. Somehow, she just knew where to go. At some time during the battle, she was wounded twice, but she never slowed down. Her honorary status was removed and she became a real United States Marine. She was promoted to Staff Sergeant.

Staff Sergeant Reckless

At the end of hostilities in Korea, Staff Sergeant Reckless was transported to Marine Corps Base Camp Pendleton in Southern California. Lieutenant General Randolph Pate USMC presented Staff Sergeant Reckless with two Purple Hearts, a Good Conduct medal, and a Presidential Unit Citation with Star. General Pate issued an order that Staff Sergeant Reckless never again carry anything heavier than her horse blanket. She retired in a grassy field at Camp Pendleton.

In 1968, she died of natural causes. She was twenty. Her remains are interred beneath a memorial to her at Camp Pendleton.

Semper Fi

Hand Salute----------Ready, Two

CHRIS KYLE

Chris Kyle was born in Odessa, Texas. His father was a Deacon, his mother a Sunday-school teacher. He grew up as a country boy; dipping tobacco, hunting deer, turkey, and quail. Most young children learning to use a firearm start with a .22 single shot rifle. On his eighth birthday, Kyle received a .30-06 rifle. By the time he was in his teens, Kyle was a professional rodeo saddle rider in local rodeos. Obviously, he loved excitement in his life. When he was old enough, he joined the U.S. Navy, with his sights on becoming a Seal. (SEa, Air, and Land)

Very few Seal applicants are accepted to attend training. Kyle was accepted and began his training. The training for most applicants lasted over a year, with a higher than ninety percent dropout rate. Kyle finished his training and earned his Special Warfare Operator Rating. During his training, his superior skills with a rifle were recognized. He was given additional training, and became a Seal sniper.

The unofficial motto of a sniper is "one shot, one kill." This bothered Kyle. He had never killed a human. The only thing he had killed were the game animals he had hunted. His first assignment was to give cover to a marine division as they entered an Iraqi town. He was hidden in an advantage point watching the marines through a Nightforce 4.5-22 mounted on a .338 Lapua Magnum rifle. He watched a women approach the marines. She had a baby in her arms. She was also holding a grenade, ready to detonate. His first kill had to be a woman. He just kept thinking about the marines and the baby that were still alive.

Chris Kyle

On another one of his four deployments to the Middle East, he was involved in the second battle for Fallujah. In that battle alone, he was credited with forty kills. The Americans gave him the nickname "The Legend." The terrorists also gave him the nickname of "Al Shatan" which means The Devil. A terrorist put a $20,000 bounty on his head. Chris said, "It just proves I'm doing my job."

In Sadr City he was credited with his longest distance-kill. He spied a man aiming a rocket launcher at an American convoy. He fired one shot from his Lapua rifle. The man fell. This shot was from a distance of over a mile. Before Chris returned to American soil, the bounty on his head had been raised to $80,000.

He had a total of 160 confirmed kills, making him the most deadly sniper in American history. Chris had been shot twice, and received multiple fragment wounds from six separate improvised explosive devices, called IEDs.

Chris Kyle retired from the navy at age thirty-seven. He took with him two Silver Stars and five Bronze Star Medals with "V"s for valor.

Hand Salute----------Ready, Two

IRENA SENDLER

Fifteen miles southwest of Warsaw, Poland is the small town of Otwock. On February 15, 1910 Otwock saw the birth of Irena Sendlerowa, who later became known as Irena Sendler. In her late teen years she became a social worker in Warsaw.

In 1939, the Germans invaded Poland and took over Warsaw. The Germans fenced off a sixteen-block area of Warsaw, nicknamed "the ghetto", and forced "the undesirables", most of which were Jews, into this area. Irena watched as hundreds of the Jews were taken from the ghetto and loaded onto trains. According to the Germans, they were destined to work in factories. She learned that the actual destination was Auschwitz where they would be murdered by lethal gas. Inside the ghetto, 5000 people a month were dying from starvation and disease. Irena had to do something.

A social worker would never be allowed access to the ghetto, but the Germans were allowing Red

Cross nurses in and out. Irena obtained some false identification and emerged as "nurse" Irena.

Gaining access to the ghetto, she found many friends she had known before the invasion. She decided to try to smuggle the infant son of a good friend out of the ghetto to avoid his fate. Irena was successful. It had worked. Irena recruited ten of her closest friends on the outside to join her, and they began removing children every day.

She got a large dog and trained him to bark wildly at any man in uniform. This not only kept away any close inspection, but the barking covered any crying by infants. She later remarked that the hardest part was to convince parents to part with their children. They asked, "Can you guarantee they'll be safe?" She responded, "I can only guarantee they'll die if they stay here." Irena found safe homes for each of the children removed, and she kept a log of names and locations of where each child had been placed.

Irena was caught one time and the Nazis broke both of her legs. Surprisingly, they released her to her friends. She later found out that she was about to be taken out and shot, but her friends had bribed her German guards. They listed her as having been executed. As soon as she was able, she jumped right back in, removing more children.

By the time Hitler was defeated, Irena and her friends had saved 2500 children. She searched for any of the parents that had survived. NONE HAD SURVIVED.

Her heroic work went mostly unrecognized until in 2007, when she was nominated for the Nobel Peace Prize. However, it was awarded to Al Gore.

Irena Sendler

On May 12, 2008 Irena Sendler passed away of pneumonia in her native Poland.

Hand Salute----------Ready, Two

VAN THOMAS BARFOOT

Van Thomas Barfoot was born on June 15, 1919 in Edinburg, Mississippi. Although he was a member of the Choctaw Nation, he never registered. Later in life, he said, "I'm not a Native American, I'm just an American".

In 1940, he joined the army. Just like everyone else starting their military service, he was a buck Private. After his basic training, he served in Louisiana, then in Puerto Rico. By December of 1941, he had been promoted to Sergeant. He was transferred to the 45th Infantry Division and was shipped to Europe.

In 1943, during the Italian campaign, he was part of the Invasion of Sicily in July, the invasion of mainland Italy at Salerno in September, and the landings at Anzio in January 1944. By May of 1944, they had pushed the enemy back to the town of Carano where the Germans took up defensive positions.

On May 23, his company attacked the German positions. Because of his patrols scouting the German's positions, he was able to lead his squad through a minefield, and was facing a German machine gun. He took out the gun with a hand grenade. Advancing, he discovered another machine gun, and killed two of the crew and captured three others of the crew. Now, he was facing yet another machine gun. He was able to capture the entire crew, and took them prisoner.

Later that same day, he observed three German Mark VI tanks advancing toward his company's position. He secured a 3.5 rocket launcher, and disabled the leading tank. The other two turned away. He captured the crew of the disabled tank. Then Sergeant Barfoot assisted three wounded American soldiers back to the relative safety of the American lines.

By the end of the day, he had killed seven enemy soldiers, and taken another seventeen as prisoners. Sergeant Barfoot was awarded the Medal of Honor for this day. He was also given a battlefield commission to Second Lieutenant.

In May of 1945, the war in Europe was won. Lieutenant Barfoot's fight with the Axis was over, but his fight for America was not.

He remained in the army and in June of 1950, now Captain Barfoot was among the first to be sent to Korea. He was a "hands on" officer and was among the last to return home in June of 1953. His fight with North Korea was over, but his fight for America was not.

In the early 1970s, faced with yet another fight for the America he loved, and now a Major, Barfoot served a full tour in Vietnam. When that war was over, his fight for America was still not done.

In 1974, the now Colonel Barfoot retired from the army. He took with him a Medal of Honor, a Silver Star, a Bronze Star, and three Purple Hearts.

Colonel Van T. Barfoot

Colonel Van Barfoot moved into a condo in Virginia, and erected a flagpole in his front yard. Each morning at 6:00 he raised Ol' Glory and saluted. At 5:00 p.m. he lowered it. The Homeowners Association (HOA) told him the flagpole was not within the association's rules, and would have to be taken down. Barfoot refused. A legal fight ensued between the HOA and Barfoot. He was able to enlist the aid of Virginia Senators Mark Warner and Jim Webb. He also was able get the backing of White House Press Secretary Robert Gibbs who lobbied the HOA on Barfoot's behalf. He won out. He continued the raising and lowering of Ol' Glory.

On March 2, 2012 at age ninety-two Van T. Barfoot's fight for America was over.

Hand Salute----------Ready, Two

RAYMOND BUTHE

In early 2012, Steve Browne had dinner at Daphne's restaurant in Lincoln, Nebraska. His change included a one-dollar bill with writing on it. When he got home, Steve made a closer inspection of the bill. It was a silver certificate that was a 1935 series. On the bill were the names Anthony DeMarco, Lt. Marvin Brawer, Sgt. John Flynn, Raymond Buthe, Lt. Charles Norris, Sgt. Ralph Coming and Lt. Curtis Chapman. The names were dated May 14, 1943 and October 22, 1944. Steve enlisted the help of his three sons, as they were more computer savvy than he was.

The four of them began an investigation that took several weeks, but little pieces began to fall into place.

Steve found that Raymond Buthe was the pilot of a B-17 Flying Fortress stationed in England. The other names on the bill made up part of his flight crew. This crew had made two successful combat flights over Germany. On November 30, 1944 they took off on their third combat mission. The target was an industrial plant in Lutzkendorf, Germany.

The flight was uneventful, but as they approached the target, the sky around them became filled with anti-aircraft fire. As the anti-aircraft fire detonated, they appeared like harmless white puffs of clouds, but these harmless white puffs of clouds contained thousands of pieces of shrapnel that projected outward at the speed of a bullet. Just one round can destroy an aircraft.

The crew successfully dropped their payload on the target, but were instantly hit by two rounds of anti-aircraft fire. The first round almost tore off the right wing, which burst into flames. The second round tore the aft section from the fuselage.

B-17 Flying Fortress

Sergeant John Flynn was in the rear of the plane and was unconscious when he was pulled out as the tail was ripped off. His parachute ripcord was attached to the interior of the plane and his chute opened automatically. He survived. John Lafferty, whose name was not listed on the dollar bills, and Curtis Chapman, successfully parachuted out. The rest of the crew died in the aircraft. All three survivors were captured and spent the duration of the war in a German POW camp.

Steve Browne discovered that the three survivors had since passed away, but he was able to locate Amy Chapman, the daughter of Curtis Chapman.

Steve has since given the signed silver certificate to Amy. She said this filled in a lot of her father's life that she had been unaware of.

Hand Salute----------Ready, Two

MAUREEN DUNLOP DE POPP

Maureen Dunlop de Popp was born on October 26, 1920 in Quilmes, Argentina. Quilmes is just outside Buenos Aires. Her father was an Australian who managed 250,000 hectares of sheep farms in Patagonia, Argentina. A hectare is a little less than a half-acre. Her mother was a British citizen. Maureen held duel citizenships, both Argentine and British. As she grew up, she developed a fascination with airplanes.

While on a vacation in England in 1936, she took flying lessons. Upon her return to Argentina, she had to lie about her age in order to continue flying.

When England got involved in World War II, there was a mass increase in the production of warplanes. Someone had to transport these planes, and the repaired planes to the Royal Air Force (RAF) airfields. An all male unit called the Air Transport Auxiliary, or ATA did transporting, up to that point. During the war, women were assuming many responsibilities that were formerly considered men's jobs. The ATA was no different.

In 1942 Maureen wanted to get involved in defending England. She joined the ATA. The pilots never knew what type of aircraft they would fly, or what their destination would be until just before that day's assignment. During her three-year tour with the ATA, Maureen flew thirty-eight different types of aircraft, including the Spitfire, Mustang, Typhoon, and the Wellington bomber. Her favorite was the Mosquito. "It's fast and nimble."

On one of her flights delivering a new Spitfire, the cockpit canopy flew off. "It was very windy." She finished the flight and landed safely. On another flight delivering a rebuilt Argus, the engine froze up. Maureen made a successful "dead stick" (without power) landing. It was discovered that a piston had shattered. In 1944 she was pictured on the cover of *Picture Post* magazine in her flying gear.

Maureen Dunlop

When Hitler was defeated, the ATA was disbanded. Maureen returned to Argentina. She instructed and flew for the Argentine Air Force. She also had a partnership in an air taxi service.

Maureen Dunlop de Popp passed away on May 29, 2012.

During the war years, the 600 pilots of the ATA delivered 308,567 aircraft, freeing the qualified male pilots to fly combat.

Hand Salute----------Ready, Two

THE BARB

In 1972 an Italian navy submarine was sold for a paltry $100,000 to be scrapped out. It's sad when any navy vessel has outlived its usefulness. You'll find this one especially sad when you know its history.

Navy surface vessels are ships, but submarines are called boats. This boat was launched April 2, 1942 and was named the USS Barb. During World War II, the Barb saw service in the Atlantic and off North Africa. She had a brief overhaul in New London, Connecticut. Then, under the command of Captain Eugene B. Fluckey, the Barb moved to the Pacific Theater.

U.S.S. Barb

On October 22 and 23 of 1944, the Barb entered Namkwan Harbor on the China coast in only thirty feet of dangerously shallow water. Capt. Fluckey found over thirty enemy ships at anchor. He fired torpedo after torpedo, damaging most of them, and sinking several. Because his top speed while submerged was only 17 kph, or 10.5 mph, and he could attain 39 kph, or 24.2 mph while surfaced, he surfaced and maneuvered through heavily mined waters making good his escape.

Captain Fluckey was awarded the Medal of Honor for this attack.

Upon receiving it, he said, "This is not mine. It belongs to every man on the Barb."

The Barb now flew a banner on its battle flag that indicated a Medal of Honor recipient was onboard.

In the air force, it's a tradition to paint a small image on the side of the victor's aircraft of the enemy aircraft that has been downed. The navy has a similar tradition. A small image of enemy ships sunk in combat is sewn onto the lower edge of the battle flag of the victor's vessel. The USS Barb had 17 enemy vessels, including a Japanese aircraft carrier, the Unyo, on its battle flag. It also had the image of a Japanese locomotive.

On July 22, 1945 the boat was on a "search and destroy" mission. This meant they were to take on targets of opportunity. They were off the east coast of Karafuto, Japan, just south of Tokyo.

The boat entered Suruga Bay. They observed a rail line with frequent supply trains going south to support Japanese troops. Captain Fluckey decided that a rail line was absolutely a target of opportunity. One of the crewmembers jerry-rigged a pressure switch so that the train itself would detonate an improvised bomb. The bomb itself was made of one of the boat's 55-pound scuttling charges. They waited four days for enough cloud cover to hide the shore party. Then eight volunteer crewmembers took two small boats to the shore. The bomb was planted. As the shore party was returning to the boat, they saw a train approaching. As the locomotive passed over the bomb, there was a tremendous explosion and the boxcars smashed into each other destroying the entire train. The USS Barb had "sunk" a train.

In 1947 the USS Barb was decommissioned and given to the Italian Navy.

Not only was this the only enemy train "sunk" by an American submarine, It was the only land invasion on Japanese home soil during all of World War II. Before he retired, Eugene B. Fluckey was promoted to Admiral.

Admiral Eugene B. Fluckey (Retired) passed away on June 28, 2007.

This is for Admiral Eugene Fluckey and the crew of the USS Barb.

Hand Salute----------Ready, Two

ABOUT THE AUTHOR

Ken Osmond was born and raised in Southern California. Throughout his early years, he was a child actor and acted in several motion pictures and many television shows. He is best known for his portrayal of Eddie Haskell on *Leave It To Beaver*.

In 1961, Ken entered the U.S. Army, and served as a small arms repairman, (gunsmith). It was a time of relative peace. He never saw combat, but is proud of his service. In 1970, he became a Los Angeles policeman.

Ken is now retired from the Screen Actors Guild and the L.A.P.D. He currently spends most of his time volunteering for the American Legion, an organization dedicated to assisting active and former military personnel.

Made in the USA
San Bernardino, CA
23 March 2014